DANTE: POET OF THE SECULAR WORLD

DANTE

POET OF THE
SECULAR WORLD

BY

ERICH AUERBACH

TRANSLATED BY

Ralph Manheim

THE UNIVERSITY OF CHICAGO PRESS

CHICAGO AND LONDON

THIS BOOK WAS ORIGINALLY PUBLISHED IN 1929 BY
WALTER DE GRUYTER & CO., BERLIN AND LEIPZIG, UNDER
THE TITLE, *Dante als Dichter der irdischen Welt*

International Standard Book Number: 0-226-03207-8 (clothbound)
Library of Congress Catalog Card Number: 61-11893

THE UNIVERSITY OF CHICAGO PRESS, CHICAGO 60637
The University of Chicago Press, Ltd., London

A NOTE ON THE TRANSLATION

The original of the present work is Auerbach's *Dante als Dichter der irdischen Welt* (Berlin and Leipzig: Verlag Walter de Gruyter, 1929). English renderings of quotations from the *Divina commedia* are regularly based on the Carlyle-Wicksteed version (Temple Classics and Modern Library), with some adjustment to minimize its archaism. A few, for similar reasons, are freshly done. Translations of the minor poems and of Dante's contemporaries, both Italian and Provençal, are all new, except when otherwise specified. For consistency and ease of consultation, the author's notes and bibliographical references have been revised in form. The translator wishes to thank Professor Theodore Silverstein of the University of Chicago for his kind and expert assistance and for much valuable advice.

CONTENTS

῍Ηθος ἀνθρώπῳ δαίμων

A man's character is his fate

I

HISTORICAL INTRODUCTION
THE IDEA OF MAN IN LITERATURE

Ever since its beginnings in Greece, European literature has possessed the insight that a man is an indivisible unity of body (appearance and physical strength) and spirit (reason and will), and that his individual fate follows from that unity, which like a magnet attracts the acts and sufferings appropriate to it. It was this insight that enabled Homer to perceive the structure of fate. He created a character—Achilles or Odysseus, Helen or Penelope —by inventing, by heaping up acts and sufferings that were all of a piece. In the poet's inventive mind an act revealing a man's nature, or, one might say, his nature as manifested in a first act, unfolded naturally and inevitably into the sum and sequence of that man's kindred acts, into a life that would take a certain direction and be caught up in the skein of events which add up to a man's character as well as his fate.

The awareness that a man's particular fate is a part of his unity, the insight embodied in the maxim of Heraclitus cited above, enables Homer to imitate real life. Here we are not referring exactly to the realism that some ancient critics praised in Homer and others found lacking in him,[1] for those critics were concerned with the probability or credibility of the events he narrates. What we have in mind is his way of narrating. Regardless of their plausibility, he makes them so clear and palpable that the question of their likelihood arises only on subsequent reflection. In the ancient view, a narrative of a fabulous or miraculous event is neces-

I

sarily unrealistic. The view I am taking here is that the portrayal can be convincing regardless of whether such a thing has ever been seen or of whether or not it is credible. We recall, for example, a Rembrandt print representing the apparition of Christ at Emmaus; it is a successful imitation of life because even an unbeliever, struck by the evidence of what he sees, is compelled to experience a miraculous event. That realism, or to cast aside a word that is ambiguous and has undergone so many changes of meaning, that art of imitation is to be met with everywhere in Homer, even when he is telling fairy tales, for the unity, the *sibi constare,* or constancy, of his figures justifies or produces the things that happen to them. In a single act the poet's fantasy creates the character and his fate. Observation and reason play a part; they enrich the scene and arrange it; but observation can do no more than register the chaotic abundance of the material, while reason tyranically cuts it to pieces, unable to keep pace with the shifting appearances. Homer's inventive gift carries within it a conviction that neither observation nor reason can wholly justify, although everything in his work supports it; the conviction that every character is at the root of his own particular fate and that he will inevitably incur the fate that is appropriate to him. But this means appropriate to him as a whole, not to any one of his attributes; for his attributes, taken in the abstract, never coincide with the figure as a whole. What can be represented in poetic terms and what demands belief on the part of the reader, is not that good things happen to a good man and brave things to a brave man, but that the fate of Achilles is Achillean; the epithets δῖος, "godlike," or πολυμῆτις, "astute," carry meaning only for those who know what they contain of Achilles' character.

Thus Homeric imitation, which the ancient critics called mimesis, is not an attempt to copy from appearance; it does not spring from observation, but like myth from the conception of figures who are all of a piece, whose unity is present even before observation begins. Their living presence and diversity stem, as we can everywhere perceive, from the situation they inevitably get involved in, and it is the situation that prescribes their actions and their sufferings. Only then, when the conception is established, does naturalistic description set in, though there is no need for the poet to summon it; it comes to him quite spontaneously. The natural truth or mimesis of a Homeric scene such as the meeting of Odysseus and Nausicaa is not based on sharp observation of daily events, but on an a priori conception of the nature and essence of both figures and the fate appropriate to them. It is that conception which creates the situation in which they meet, and once the conception is there, the narrative that will transform the fiction into truth follows of its own accord. Thus Homer's portraiture is no mere copy of life, not only because he tells stories that could never happen in real life but because he has a conception of man that experience alone could not have given him.

Tragedy grew out of the epic myth; but in developing a form of its own, distinct from the epic, it concentrated more and more on the actual decision; a man and his destiny are laid bare in the moment when they become wholly and irrevocably one—the moment of doom. In Homeric epic a man moves toward his fate in a gradual process of clarification and the hero's end need not necessarily come into the story. Classical tragedy, on the other hand, discloses the end of his career, when he has left all diversity behind him and no escape is possible; deciphered and manifest, his disastrous fate stands there before him like a stranger; fear grips his innermost being; he tries to defend himself against the universal which is destined to engulf his individual life; he flings himself into the hopeless final struggle against his own daemon. That struggle, which stands out most clearly in Sophocles, is such that those who enter into it lose a part of their individual nature; they are so caught up in their extreme plight, so carried away by the final struggle, that nothing remains of their personality but their age, sex, position in life, and the most general traits of their temperament; their actions, their words and gestures are wholly governed by the dramatic situation, that is, by the tactical requirements of their struggle. Nevertheless, Greek tragedy left its hero a good deal of his individuality; especially in the opening scene, when he still stands there firm and intact, he shows the particular, contingent, earthly side of himself with reality and dignity; and even later on, after the breach between his individuality and his fate, when the universality of his fate becomes more and more manifest, he still retains, whether convulsively clinging to it or heroically sacrificing it, the characteristic form of his vital will. But here there is no place for the epic spontaneity which at every moment derives colorful new forms from the concordance of the two elements of his unity. Formerly, in his epic life, man's individuality was enriched by each new turn of his fate, but here he has grown hard and rigid and poor in color and detail. He resists his all too universal doom, yet runs to meet it; all that remains of him is what is most universal, a man on the way to his doom, squandering and exhausting his store of vital energy, which can no longer bear fruit.

In the Sophist Enlightenment the character lost its unity; psychological analysis and a rational interpretation of events dispersed the compelling power of destiny. The form of the tragedy was preserved only with the help of technical devices: often an arbitrary, empty, and mechanical plot contrasted irritatingly with subtle psychological perception. At the same time comedy with its observation and imitation of daily life, its rationalist caricatures, just or unjust, of everything that was unusual, began, though with ups and downs, to gain the support of the enlightened public and to discredit the notion of a priori unity of character.

That was the situation when Plato developed his critique of imitative art. Plato scorned his own feeling for sensuous reality and his own poetic talent, and in his conception of a strict, pure utopia, condemned the indiscriminate emotion aroused by art. The results of his long meditations on the subject are set forth in the tenth book of the *Republic:* if the empirical world is second in rank, a deceptive copy of the Ideas, which alone have truth and being, then art, which concerns itself with the imitation of appearance, is still lower in the scale, a clouded, inferior copy of a copy, third in respect to truth: $\tau\rho\iota\tau o\nu$ $\tau\iota$ $\dot{a}\pi\dot{o}$ $\tau\hat{\eta}s$ $\dot{a}\lambda\eta\theta\epsilon\iota as;$[2] it is addressed to the lower, irrational part of the soul; there poetry and philosophy have always been in conflict, and poetry must be excluded from the philosophical Republic. He grants a limited value to the non-imitative arts, which are disciplined by a firm tradition and make no concession to changing, deceptive appearances; they, he holds, can serve to fortify civic virtue in the philo-

4

sophical state. But that only underlines his basic condemnation of all truly creative art.

However, Plato's teachings did not destroy the dignity of imitative art—on the contrary, they gave it a new impulse that was to endure for many centuries and assigned it a new aim. Not that Plato was not serious in his view. Neither his praises of inspiration in other dialogues, nor the mimetic art he himself practised so consummately and for which indeed he was criticized,[3] can alter our belief that this passage represents his essential attitude which, despite his own poetic disposition, despite dangerous trials and temptations, had taken form in the pure perfection of his theory of ideas. Yet the influence of his words was colored by the memory of the man who had spoken them. In various ways he had praised phenomenal beauty as a stage on the way to true beauty; it was through him that artists and lovers of art first began to reflect on the presence of the Idea in the appearance of things and to yearn for it. It was Plato who bridged the gap between poetry and philosophy; for, in his work, appearance, despised by his Eleatic and Sophist predecessors, became a reflected image of perfection. He set poets the task of writing philosophically, not only in the sense of giving instruction, but in the sense of striving, by the imitation of appearance, to arrive at its true essence and to show its insufficiency measured by the beauty of the Idea. He himself understood the art of mimesis more profoundly and practised it more consummately than any other Greek of his time, and apart from Homer he had greater influence as a poet than any other poet of antiquity. The figures in his dialogues are represented in their innermost individuality; the dialogue itself is shot through with movement and actuality; the most abstract disquisition becomes a work of magic, whose sensuous color, in every receptive mind, merges with the subject matter and seems to become one with it. It is false, indeed it is quite impossible, to look upon the poetry in Plato as a kind of subterfuge or delusion from which we must free ourselves in order to arrive at the true meaning of his thought. Plato's love of the particular was his way to wisdom, the way described in Diotima's monologue. It achieved such unique expression because for him man's universal τέλος, or end, did not conflict with the individual nature and

5

destiny of men, but was shaped and expressed in them. That unity of essence and destiny is set forth in the myth recounted by Er the Pamphylian who stood before the throne of Lachesis and beheld how the souls of the dead chose their destinies before returning to new life[4]—for each soul retained its individual character, which death had not destroyed. Plato's art is pious; it is a supreme expression, confirmed and purified by reason, of the mythical consciousness of destiny. Herein and in the power of the soul to partake of the beauty of the Idea, the dualism of the Platonic system is transcended. The influence of this Plato, who introduced philosophy into art and laid the foundations for a more profound and at the same time more accurate perception of events, lived on in the minds of future generations. The enriched perception embodied in his art also springs from his philosophical attitude. In the dialogue form that he created there is, strictly speaking, no encounter with fate, no dramatic situation; even in the Socrates trilogy—the *Apology, Crito, Phaedo*—the encounter with fate is no more than a background. In its place truth becomes the judge; in the quiet movement of the dialogue, men of all ages pass before the judgment seat of truth, constrained, like the souls passing before the judges of the underworld in the myth that Socrates relates at the end of the *Gorgias*,[5] to lay bare their willingness, devotion, resolution. Here the soul must prove its courage and nobility, its inherent truth, as the body must prove its strength and skill in an athletic contest, and although these secret, intangible things are disclosed in terms of appearance, of the most manifest sense perception, they seem at the same time to be weighed in scales of the utmost precision and defined as it were by an art of measurement.

Thus it is not surprising that the philosophical theory of art should find not its end but its beginning in the Platonic critique of imitation. The theory of Ideas in itself contained the germ of a transformation whose significance for the fine arts has recently been set forth by E. Panofsky.[6] Then, little by little, thinkers concerned with a philosophical justification of the arts moved the Platonic Ideas or archetypes, from the supra-celestial realm to the soul, from the transcendent to the immanent world. The object which the artist imitated underwent a similar change, passing from the empirical world to the soul, for it was held that what the artist imitated could not be the real object—for if it were, the work of art would not be more beautiful than the immediate object—but the image in his soul, which is nothing other than the immanent Idea, the ἐννόημα. Now the imitated object and the truth, which Plato had distinguished so sharply, met in the soul of the artist, and the higher perfection which to Plato's mind could be encountered only in the supra-celestial realm, was imputed to the immanent Idea in contrast with actuality and, later on, with the work itself as well. Consequently the notion of mimesis underwent an extreme spiritualization which, though rooted in Plato's theory of Ideas, produced a result diametrically opposed to Plato's teachings, that is, a belief in the sublimity of art; and ultimately—in Plotinus, who accentuated the contrast between the archetype in the soul of the creative artist and the materialized work, which could never be anything but a veiled copy—this same process gave rise to a new dualism and a new problem.

The first important step in this revision and application to art of the theory of Ideas is Aristotle's aesthetics: its influence on the historical development of the theory is great, but it is less significant than the Platonic theory itself for those who seek to investigate the respective parts played by sensibility and metaphysics in actual works of art. The doctrine of the self-realization of the essence in the phenomenon, whereby the individual formed thing becomes reality and substance, gave imitation a new philosophical justification; all the more so since Aristotle, in his formulation of change, or process, as the entrance of form into matter, had in mind human artistic creation as well as the organic process. In artistic activity, the form, the εἶδος, is in the soul of the artist, and herein we see the relevance to the theory of art of the above-mentioned transference of the Ideas to the immanent world. Accordingly Aristotle, in opposition to Plato, expressly defends poetry as a *poietic* philosophy, which in tragedy, its highest form, arouses and overcomes certain emotions, and thus, far from being harmful and demoralizing, purifies the soul. Tragedy is thus more philosophical than historiography, which is a pure copying of events, because in tragedy the individual gives way to

7

the universal, and contingency to probability. Thus Aristotle, by his doctrine that the Idea is actualized in the formed particular, rehabilitated the formed particular as an object worthy to be imitated. But since, opposite to the creative εἶδος of the artist, the formed object reverts to matter, it follows that the artistic imitation is more perfectly formed than its empirical model and hence higher in rank. These principles, however, spring solely from rational insight into the individual occasion, not from participation in its essence, not from the process, that Plato must have experienced, of losing oneself in reality and finding oneself again. Aristotle did not try to fathom the part of actuality which resists rational formulation, but dropped it as having neither law nor purpose. To his mind what could not be explained was mere contingency, the inevitable resistance of matter, and as such occupied the bottommost rank in his metaphysical order of the universe. Compared to the dualism of Plato's "two worlds," this dualism of form and matter seems easily bridged—for each empirical thing points to the process by which it will be transcended. But when applied to events, it implies—and indeed this is the conception underlying Aristotle's ethics—that something utterly contingent and alien can befall man; for what reason cannot resolve is τὸ οὐχ ἄνευ, or the *sine qua non,* of pure matter, or contingency. Such a conception is only natural to a man of Aristotle's cast of mind, who judges destiny by the rational concept of justice, but —quite unlike Plato's doctrine of two worlds, which dismissed happening as illusion, yet left room for the mythical illumination of happening—it is diametrically opposed to the tragic view of fate. Certain of Aristotle's ideas concerning the poet's relation to real happening, as set forth in the *Poetics,* follow from this attitude. He states very clearly that reality must not be represented as it comes to us, in its apparent disorder and disunity, and his view in this matter was taken as a norm for centuries to come. To his mind the disorder and disunity of actual happening do not stem from the inadequacy of the eyes that look upon it, but are present in happening itself, so that the poet must create a happening superior to actual happening and tragedy must present a correction of actual events. Thus he opposes the universality of poetry to the particularity of history and expressly bases the unity of tragedy not on the hero, who can be assailed by disparate events, but on the rationalized fable which, he declares, can be independent of the character. This view led Aristotle to a system in which poetic possibilities are almost too rigidly departmentalized and restricted; it exerted a decisive influence on subsequent theory and by and large marks a limit which the poetics of the ancients was never to surpass. The only significant exception is Plato; we recall the richly meaningful scene at the end of the *Symposium,* in which Socrates tries to explain to Agathon and Aristophanes, both half-asleep, that one and the same man ought to be capable of writing both comedies and tragedies.[7]

A rationalistic negation of fate was the prevailing attitude of antiquity from Aristotle to the triumph of Christianity and the mystery religions; that was just as true of the Stoics who, in their necessary order of the world, equated reason with nature, as of the Epicureans with their metaphysical concept of freedom; and both those philosophies culminated in an ethical ideal which insulated the individual against his fate. The wise man is he whose equanimity nothing can disturb; he overcomes the outside world by refusing to participate in it, by subduing his emotions.

Late Greek rationalism is the dominant attitude in the Roman poetry and poetic theory of the Golden Age; that applies to Cicero as well as to Horace or Seneca. Only where the destiny and mission of Rome were involved, in Virgil and in Tacitus, did the creative imagination overcome the fatelessness inherent in the philosophical style of the age, and then there emerged an image of actuality as an a priori unity. Virgil has been greatly misunderstood and underestimated by the younger generation in Germany; the fault lies in a comparison with Homer based on two misconceptions; on the one hand these young men rashly identify Homer with a primitive stage of development, while on the other they distrust Virgil because of the over-cultivated, "classicist" period in which he lived, as though more refined conditions of life and liberation from crude anthropomorphic forms of religion were a fundamental obstacle to poetic creation. That prejudice has blinded many men's hearts to the consummate magic of Virgil's poetry, its purity of feeling, and above all to the spiritual rebirth it betokens. This peasant's son from northern

Italy, whom the most reserved of his contemporaries and even the political leaders of the day regarded as a favorite of nature and looked upon with a kind of loving awe, combined a deep attachment to the Italian soil with the highest culture of his time. Those two elements were so fused in him that his rural traditionalism seems to be the quintessence of a perfect culture, while his cultivation gives the impression of a profound natural wisdom, at once earthly and divine. The experience of his youth and an intuitive sense of the forces at work in his time combined to mold in him a belief in the impending rebirth of the world. Seen in terms of the philosophy of history, the fourth Eclogue, in which he celebrates the birth of the child and the dawn of a new era, this poem of inspired learning which encompasses the eschatological conceptions of all the civilized peoples of the ancient world, really has the significance that the sage error of the Middle Ages attributed to it. What utterly distinguishes Virgil's conception from all the eschatological traditions he employs,[8] is not merely his art, with which he raises the obscure, scattered, subterranean and secret wisdom of the Hellenistic Mediterranean countries to the broad light of day; it is rather the fact that for him all that dark wisdom took on a concrete form in the hoped-for and already dawning world order of the Imperium. These are the roots of his poetic and prophetic power. The character and the fate of the pious Aeneas, who out of affliction and confusion made his way through temptation and danger toward his allotted destiny, were something new to ancient literature. The idea that a man should pursue a definite sacred mission in the earthly world was unknown to the Homeric epics; ascent through many degrees of trial was indeed a familiar motif in the Orphic and Pythagorean mysteries, but it was never connected with a concrete career on earth. Aeneas is conscious of his mission; it was revealed to him by the prophecy of his divine mother and by the words of his father in the underworld, and he takes it upon himself with proud piety. The prophecies of Anchises and the glorification of the Julian line may strike us as insipid flattery, but only because Virgil's formula has too often been abused for unworthy and trivial purposes. Virgil's view of the world follows the truth of historical development as he saw it, and it endured and exerted an influence far longer than he could have foreseen; he was indeed a kind of prophet, or else the word has lost its meaning. And into the history of the world he wove the first great love story in a form that remains valid to this day. Though not successful in every detail, as a whole it is a masterpiece and for the European literature of love, a basic model. Dido suffers more deeply and poignantly than Calypso, and her story is the one example of great sentimental poetry known to the Middle Ages.

Thus for European literature Virgil was in many respects an important innovator, and his influence extended far beyond literature. He was the mythologist of Europe's most characteristic political form, the creative synthetist of Roman and Hellenistic eschatologies, and the first poet of sentimental love. He was the first of his cultural sphere to transcend the fatelessness of late Greek philosophy and to see the a priori unity of the character in his fate. True, there is an uncertainty in his theological attitude, for what he glorified was an earthly institution, and the union of religious currents that he exploited poetically aimed at more than that; in his picture of the other world—an after-life at the service of Rome's greatness—the traditional doctrines of purification and transmigration are not developed quite consistently; his realm of the dead is merely an artistic instrument, and as in all the ancient conceptions, the souls of the departed have only a partial, diminished life, a shadowy existence.

The historical core of Christianity—that is to say, the Crucifixion and the related events—offers a more radical paradox, a wider range of contradiction, than anything known to the ancient world, either in its history or in its mythical tradition. The fantastic march of the man from Galilee and his action in the temple, the sudden crisis and catastrophe, the pitiful derision, the scourging and crucifixion of the King of the Jews, who only a short time before had wished to proclaim the Kingdom of God on earth, the despairing flight of the disciples, and then the apotheosis, based on the visions of a few men, perhaps of only one, a fisherman from the lake of Gennesaret—this entire episode, which was to provoke the greatest of all transformations in the inner and outward history of our civilized world, is astonishing in every respect. Even today, anyone who tries to form a clear picture of what happened is deeply puzzled; he cannot but feel that myth and dogma gained only a relative ascendancy in the books of the New Testament and that the paradoxical, disharmonious, perplexing character of those events erupts at every turn.

The frequently adduced comparison[9] with the death of Socrates helps to bring out our meaning. Socrates, too, died for what he believed and he died of his own free will. He could have saved himself; he could have escaped before his trial or taken a less intransigent attitude at it, or have fled afterwards. But he did not wish to: serene and untroubled, he died surrounded by his friends, the earthly dignity of his person undiminished; this was the death of a philosopher and of a happy man, whose destiny seems to confirm and fulfil our human sense of justice; his enemies are anonymous figures, representing the special interests of the moment, of little importance to their contemporaries and of none at all to posterity; the fact that they held the power merely gave Socrates a last welcome occasion to fulfil and reveal himself.

Jesus, on the other hand, unleashed a movement which by its very nature could not remain purely spiritual; his followers, who recognized him as the Messiah, expected the immediate coming of the Kingdom of God on earth. And all that was a lamentable failure. The multitude, on whom he must for a moment have exerted a considerable influence, remained in the end hesitant or hostile; the ruling groups joined forces against him; he was compelled to hide at night outside the city, and in his hiding place he was finally betrayed by one of those closest to him, arrested in the midst of confused and vacillating disciples, and brought before the Sanhedrin. And now the worst of all: the disciples despaired and fled, and Peter, the root and eternal head of Christendom, denied him. Alone, he faced the judges and suffered his disgraceful martyrdom, while the multitude was permitted to mock him in the most cruel way: of all his followers, only a few women witnessed his end from afar.

Harnack[10] called Peter's denial of Christ "that terrible leftward swing of the pendulum" and believed that in conjunction with the memory of the transfiguration (Mark 8: 27–29), it provided the psychological basis for the vision of St. Peter on which the Church was founded, for it may, he says, "have resulted in an equally violent swing to the right." But the denial and vision of Peter, this evident paradox, are only the most conspicuous example of the contradictory character that dominates the story of Jesus from the beginning. From the very first it moves between malignant scoffers and boundless believers, in an atmosphere strangely compounded of the sublime and the ridiculous; the admiration and emulation of his disciples do not prevent them from misunderstanding him frequently, and their relations with him are marked by constant unrest and tension.

In entering into the consciousness of the European peoples, the story of Christ fundamentally changed their conceptions of man's fate and how to describe it. The change occurred very slowly, far more slowly than the spread of Christian dogma. It faced other obstacles that were harder to overcome: resistances which, insignificant in themselves, were impervious to the political and tactical factors that favored the acceptance of Christianity, because they were rooted in the most conservative element of a people's being, namely the innermost sensory ground of their view of the world. To that view of the world the apparatus of Christian dogma could be adapted more easily and quickly than could the spirit of the events from which it had grown. But before we enter into the history of this change and the phenomena it produced in the course of time, let us try to describe the nature of the change.

The story of Christ is more than the *parousia* of the *logos,* more than the manifestation of the idea. In it the idea is subjected to the problematic character and desperate injustice of earthly happening. Considered in itself that is, without the posthumous and never fully actualized triumph in the world, as the mere story of Christ on earth, it is so hopelessly terrible that the certainty of an actual, concretely tangible correction in the hereafter remains the only issue, the only salvation from irrevocable despair. Consequently, Christian eschatological conceptions took on an unprecedented concreteness and intensity; this world has meaning only in reference to the next; in itself it is a meaningless torment. But the otherworldly character of justice did not, as it would have where the classical spirit prevailed, detract from the

13

value of earthly destiny or from man's obligation to submit to it. The Stoic or Epicurean withdrawal of the philosopher from his destiny, his endeavor for release from the chain of earthly happening, his determination to remain at least inwardly free from earthly ties—all that is completely un-Christian. For to redeem fallen mankind the incarnated truth had subjected itself without reserve to earthly destiny. That was the end of the eudaemonism which was the foundation of ancient ethics: as Christ had taught by his presence on earth, it was the Christian's duty to do atonement and suffer trials by taking destiny upon himself, by submitting to the sufferings of the creature. The drama of earthly life took on a painful, immoderate, and utterly un-classical intensity, because it is at once a wrestling with evil and the foundation of God's judgment to come. In diametrical opposition to the ancient feeling, earthly self-abnegation was no longer regarded as a way from the concrete to the abstract, from the particular to the universal. What presumption to strive for theoretical serenity when Christ himself lived in continuous conflict! Inner tension was insuperable, and, like acceptance of earthly destiny, a necessary consequence of the story of Christ. In both cases man's individuality is humbled, but it is, and must be, preserved. Not only is Christian humility far more compelling and more concrete, one might almost say more worldly, than Stoic apathy, but through awareness of man's inevitable sinfulness, it also does far more to intensify man's awareness of his unique, inescapable personality. And the story of Christ revealed not only the intensity of personal life but also its diversity and the wealth of its forms, for it transcended the limits of ancient mimetic aesthetics. Here man has lost his earthly dignity; everything can happen to him, and the classical division of genres has vanished; the distinction between the sublime and the vulgar style exists no longer. In the Gospels, as in ancient comedy, real persons of all classes make their appearance: fishermen and kings, high priests, publicans, and harlots participate in the action; and neither do those of exalted rank act in the style of classical tragedy, nor do the lowly behave as in a farce; quite on the contrary, all social and aesthetic limits have been effaced. On that stage there is room for all human diversity, whether we consider the cast of characters as a

whole or each character singly; each individual is fully legitimated, but not on any social grounds; regardless of his earthly
position, his personality is developed to the utmost, and what befalls him is neither sublime nor base; even Peter, not to mention
Jesus, suffers profound humiliation. The depth and scope of the
naturalism in the story of Christ are unparalleled; neither the
poets nor the historians of antiquity had the opportunity or the
power to narrate human events in that way.

We have already said, and indeed it is well known though seldom stated in this connection, that the mimetic content of the
story of Christ required a very long time, more than a thousand
years, to enter into the consciousness of the faithful, even of the
peoples early converted to Christianity, and to reshape their view
of destiny. What first penetrated the minds of men was the doctrine, but in the course of the struggle with other revealed religions, with Hellenistic rationalism and the myths of the barbarian peoples, the doctrine itself underwent a change and even
the story of Christ was resorbed in a sense by the shifting requirements of the struggle. The necessity of adapting it to the mental-
ity of various peoples to which the doctrine was carried in polem-
ics or missionary sermons involved a number of metamorphoses,
each one of which destroyed a fragment of its concrete reality, and
in the end little remained of the doctrine but a sequence of dogmatic abstractions. But the reality was never wholly lost; the
gravest threat came early, from Neo-Platonic Spiritualism and
its Christian heresies, and once that was overcome, what was
essential was saved.

The Hellenistic melting pot, in which the oriental mystery religions converged, was too much imbued with Neo-Platonic
spirituality to accept the incarnation of God in its concrete historical or mythical form; the whole story underwent a reinterpretation. The events and persons were transformed into astral or
metaphysical symbols; the historical element lost its autonomy
and inherent meaning, and became a foundation for an elaborate
rationalistic speculation, which derived a kind of eerie reality, an
equivocal apocalyptic profundity, from the barely discernible vestiges of the original narrative. Even in its purest forms Neo-
Platonism took a complex and unproductive attitude toward the

empirical world, its reality, and the possibility of representing it in art. In the aesthetics of Plotinus, elements of Platonic and Aristotelian metaphysics, fused with his own emanationism and inclination toward mystical, synthetic contemplation, give rise to the idea of an earthly beauty in which the spirit participates; but beauty is pure only in the inner archetype, for in this conception the Aristotelian notion of a matter not fully formed, equated with the Platonic $\mu\grave{\eta}$ $\check{o}\nu$, or non-being, becomes the metaphysical counterpole of the Idea, which alone has full being. Thus matter ceases to mean mere resistance and, because of its diversity and divisibility, takes on the quite non-Aristotelian sense of evil. Despite the emanation of the spirit into the physical world, the manifold and concrete (through *physis,* which here becomes the *principium individuationis,* signifying the lower soul) become once again evil and impure. Accordingly, the mimetic art loses all contact with empirical reality and becomes pure $\epsilon\H{\nu}\rho\epsilon\sigma\iota\varsigma$, a copying of the inner form. Even as Plotinus provided the theoretical foundation of all spiritualist systems of aesthetics; the practical consequence, with his insistence on the superiority of being to becoming, of idea and matter, and his identification of matter and change with metaphysical non-being, was to demolish all possibility of representing earthly destiny in art.

Beside that destruction of the phenomenal world, the hostility of the Church Fathers to art was almost insignificant; for such hostility was directed only against particular themes and attitudes, and not fundamentally against the world of appearance. From such a negation of appearance the Church Militant was saved by the earthly event with which it had begun and which, with its own unquestioned reality, lent meaning and order to all appearances. Not without dogmatic obfuscation but with a consistent tenacity, the Western Church, in opposition to spiritualist influence, held fast to the life of Christ on earth as a concrete event, as the central fact of history, and conceived of history as a true record of the relations of human individuals with one another and with God. In the East, spiritualist views soon gained the upper hand and transformed the life of Christ into a triumphal rite. In the West it seemed for a moment as though a mimetic attitude toward the Gospel story, based on direct experience of its gripping reality, were about to emerge; at least the groundwork for such a development is present in the dramatic thinking of Augustine. For Augustine managed to save a good deal from the spiritualism of the Neo-Platonists and Manichaeans: by his analytical investigation of consciousness, he preserved the unity of the personality; with his metaphysical speculation, he saved the idea of a personal God; and in his teleological history of the world he saved the reality of earthly happening. The very way in which he formulated the problem of free will and predestination bears witness to the fundamentally European determination not to abolish reality by speculation, not to take flight into transcendence, but to come to grips with the real world and master it. In Augustine the history of salvation is taken concretely, and that is why, as Harnack once wrote,[11] he is able to endow Latin and the future tongues of Europe with "a Christian soul and the language of the heart."

Yet even in the West the concrete power of the Gospel story remained for a long time ineffectual. The necessity of communicating the Christian message to the barbarian tribes that were pouring into the Empire coincided with the cultural task of Romanization; and since Christian and classical myth were equally alien and incomprehensible to barbarians, the ideas and sensuous images of Hellenistic culture underwent an often violent reinterpretation, which completely destroyed the already impaired sensibility of the ancient peoples and at the same time combated and numbed the sensibility inherent in the barbaric myths. Neo-Platonic tendencies and popular mysticism had the same effect: sensibility disintegrated and there arose a debased, vulgar form of spiritualism which could neither apprehend nor give form to the phenomenal world. That situation was not first brought on by the actual migrations; in Italy the beginnings of a vulgar spiritualism under oriental influence are already apparent in the first and second centuries. Here however—in the Christian sarcophagi and catacomb paintings—symbolism is not yet used for a rationalist reinterpretation and explanation of a foreign doctrine, but serves to remind those possessing a secret knowledge of a truth that is their very own: This picture writing, illustrating a prayer for the dead, preserves, if not the concrete reality itself, at least an authentic memory of it. Later on that was to change. To the barbarian peoples of Western Europe, the complex Mediterranean culture, charged with so many historical presuppositions, was radically alien and unassimilable; it was much easier for them to take over existing institutions and dogmas, than to assimilate the concrete historical images from which they had grown. The images did not disappear; they were too closely bound up with the institutions and dogmas adopted by the barbarians for that; but they lost their character of concrete reality and became didactic allegories. The entire tradition of the ancient world, Christian as well as pagan, was thus reinterpreted in terms of vulgar spiritualism; the actual event lost its independent value, the tradition concerning it lost its literal meaning; every event recorded in the tradition came to mean something other than itself, a lesson or dogma; the concrete reality was lost. The consequence was a rather dismal sort of erudition; elements of astrology, mystical doctrine, Neo-Platonism, strangely distorted in the vulgar mind, were summoned up in support of this reinterpretation of events, and an abstruse art of allegorical exegesis was born.

The historiography of the early Middle Ages shows how men's perception of concrete reality, even of contemporary events, had been blunted. Most of the Romanized Gothic and Frankish chroniclers were utterly unable to deal with the welter of events taking place around them. Their accounts are crude; the psychological insight of late antiquity was baffled by the primitive instincts at work in the contemporary struggles for power, and one violent event follows another in a series without character or relief. Over the whole flutters a spiritual preoccupation quite irrelevant to the material in hand; for spiritualism had become a threadbare rationalism, manifested for example in the conviction that God would help the true believers to victory and defeat the heathen and the heretics. The inflexible dogmatists, lacking either cultural refinement or a mythical sense of destiny, were quite unable to interpret events and weave them into a living whole. They make no attempt to connect their point of view with the material but merely state it from time to time, in the introduction or wherever convenient, and otherwise let events run along as they please. Or else the chronicler may not even try to provide a historical record and merely reinterprets events to suit himself in a series of dry, didactic fables. Writers of sermons and religious literature had an easier time of it. Here nothing stood in the way of allegorical interpretation, and every object and event was endowed with a "meaning," which was unrelated to its actual character but clung to it like a title. And it should also be stressed that despite or perhaps because of the difficulty they had in expressing themselves, many of the writers of the sixth and seventh centuries reverted to the artificial rhetorical style of Asianism.

In the course of a very slow development which it is hard to follow, the power to depict sensuous reality revived. European Christendom emerged from the struggles of the second half of the first millennium as a new *orbis terrarum;* and here the history of Christ operated unremittingly, day after day, as a force for unity. It became the creative myth of the nations, rekindling men's perception of the world and drawing all other traditions into its sphere. And in the end that history, in which reality and meaning are so peculiarly one, in which the miraculous is so manifest and close at hand, overcame the spectral vestiges of the Platonic doctrine of two worlds. In the mimetic revival that now took place in the liturgy, imitation is no longer separate from the truth; the sensory appearance is divine and the event is the truth. That re-emergence of appearance and event was the true innovation in the culture of Western Europe, the source of the peculiarly youthful quality which soon began to distinguish it from its more purely spiritualist oriental models. The real event recaptured its legendary aura and became, with all its spiritual dignity and miraculous power, a part of daily experience; that is the naturalism of the early Middle Ages. It culminated in a spirituality which encompassed the whole of earthly life at every level, the great political developments no less than men's occupations and domestic activities, the seasons and the hours of the day. The creative energies of the barbaric peoples were suffused with the spirituality of the history of Christ; it enlisted in its service the myths growing out of the barbarian migrations, and ordered them into a unified picture of a meaningful life. Thus toward the end of the first millennium vulgar spiritualism was freed from rigid dogmatism. It became a universal and universally present spiritualization of the earthly world which however retained its patent sensuous reality; it gave the great political struggles their meaning and motive force. Human destiny and the history of the world became once more an object of direct and compelling experience, for in the great drama of salvation every man is present, acting and suffering; he is directly involved in everything that has happened and that happens each day. No escape is possible from this thoroughly spiritual and yet real earthly world, from an individual fate that is decisive for all eternity.

On that foundation the mimetic art of the Middle Ages came into being. It aimed directly at the concrete representation of transcendent substance; this involvement of naturalism and spiritualism has perhaps been described most completely and eloquently by Dvořák in his work on idealism and naturalism in Gothic sculpture and painting,[12] and its best known contemporary formulation is the saying of Suger of Saint-Denis: *mens hebes ad verum per materialia surgit* (The dull mind rises to the truth by way of material things). But the spiritualization of the world went far beyond the Church and the strictly religious sphere; it encompassed institutions and events which, by their nature and origin, would not seem to have lent themselves to such illumination. It incorporated the wild, crude power of the heroic legends, turned the feudal system into a symbolic hierarchy, and transformed God into the supreme feudal overlord. It interpreted the heroes as crusaders, linked their warlike deeds with the pilgrimage routes, and from Roland's death at Ronceval created the paradox of the warrior martyr, to whom death in battle means transcendent fulfillment. Thus a conception of the perfect man grew from the ideas of vulgar spiritualism, and perhaps it has never been sufficiently stressed how profoundly that romantic ideal is rooted in antiquity. The notions generally associated with "ancient" and "Christian" are still too one-sided; antiquity is not synonymous with worldly materialism, and it is far from being sufficiently recognized that what Europe inherited directly from antiquity is not the culture of Attic Greece or the pragmatic spirit of the Romans, but the cloudy syncretistic Neo-Platonism merged with Christianity, for which we have coined the term "vulgar spiritualism." The "ideal" of the Christian

20

knight of the chivalric epics is a product of Neo-Platonism; in the finest poems that it inspired, particularly in Wolfram's *Parzival*,[13] the authentic ideality of great European poetry found its first complete embodiment; the epic diversity of characters and their fates is preserved, but the unity of the poem resides in a Platonic ascent to purification and sanctification, which is here wonderfully blended with Germanic motivations. Here we have an irradiation of earthly existence, by which even the most particular and time-bound form of life becomes a noble incarnation of the spirit, worthy to be disclosed in epic detail. But the profoundest effect of medieval spirituality was the new attitude toward earthly love, which first made its appearance in Provence and radically influenced all subsequent European literature.

The praise and transfiguration of the beloved occur in all love poetry; they spring from the very nature of sensual ecstasy, which modifies, or rather wholly eliminates, the customary aspect of reality and permits the lover to perceive only the object of his desire and what pertains to it. But, up to the time of the troubadours, love poetry in the strict sense had never expressed anything other than sensual desire in all its variants, never praised anything but the material qualities of its object; the poets of love had always been conscious of treating a light theme unrelated to man's serious concerns and unfit for sublime poetry; they had regarded their love, real or feigned, as a mere pleasure that would soon pass, or else as a pathological, unnatural state. But here for the first time in Europe sensuous desire blended with the metaphysical foundations of a culture. Scholars have shown how much Provençal culture owed to ecclesiastical conceptions, to the cult of the Virgin, to feudal institutions; oriental and Arabic influences have been unearthed, and earlier centers of courtly refinement have been adduced. But in the last analysis all this—not to mention the parallels with Ovid that are so often cited—is mere material; for the spirit of that brief cultural flowering is quite unique. The country itself and its ethnic mixture, the cultural undercurrents that had come down from the days of the Greek colonies, the intense but not yet destructive spiritual and political movements that poured in from East and West toward the turn of the twelfth century—such imponderables assuredly played a

larger part than any specific influences. The essential fact is
Provence itself: the enchanted landscape and a mode of life that
had grown up in harmony with it. That was what gave the poets
their love of country and sense of election, their taste for adventure, and their feeling for the mysterious magic of formed reality;
that was what gave them the force to transform mere didactic
allegory into a new vision of reality. But force and vision were
both essentially Neo-Platonic; the force is Eros, Love, and the
vision is a spiritual reality which gives form to life. Gone was the
obscure, far-fetched, pedantic reinterpretation of the sensory
world; the unified culture which here rose above vulgar spiritualism sprang from a sure, direct perception; it was perception that
gave rise to the ideal—closely related to the mystical synthesis of
Neo-Platonism—of the perfect, well-formed life devoted to the
service of love. The Provençal poets compounded spirit and flesh
in a poetic vision; their creation is more fragile and artificial,
more limited than that of the Greeks; it was a "second" youth
that had to absorb much that was old before it could take on a
life of its own; and it was inseparably bound to the καιρός, the
unique moment, to a very particular and therefore short-lived
society.

But even in its fragility, that ethos created an ultimate which
was to be its gift to the world. From the over-stylized experience
of love and from the *sirventes,* the satirical poems with which the
Provençal spirit sought to defend itself against the incursion of
formlessness, sprang the dialectical play of the *trobar clus,* the
confessions in ciphered language, the passionate paradoxes, to use
Rudolf Borchardt's[14] expressive phrase. The penchant to dialectical games, characteristic of all medieval spiritualism, was inborn
in the Provençals, and Guilhem de Peitieu, the earliest of the
troubadours, already took this tone. But only when the courtly
ethos was beginning to decline, in Peire d'Alvernhe, Giraut de
Bornelh, and above all in Arnaut Daniel, does the paradoxical
riddle become the actual vehicle of meaning, and thereby the
root of a great tradition. Here again we have allegory; but the
riddles are not interpreted, and perhaps they do not even contain
any intelligible general idea that can be interpreted for all. In a
defensive, esoteric form, as though behind high walls, they hold

the endangered secret form of the soul; what was first a game and then a defense, became the refuge of a dwindling élite, and in the end an expression of the inner cleavage of a soul striving, in an allegorical dialectic, to master the torment of passion. But at that point the *trobar clus* broke through the narrow frame of the Provençal cultural sphere; there is the bridge to the *dolce stil nuovo* and to Dante.

II

DANTE'S EARLY POETRY

The Provençal poets made their songs for a particular and very limited social group; the form of life they reflect was valid only for the members of that class; they alone understood and appreciated this markedly esoteric game of love, with its set terminology and radically unpopular idiom. But from the very start great Provençal poetry was distinguished from any popular art by something more than its sociological characteristics. There was a second principle of selection based directly on human and cultural form. That is what gives the Provençal poets their distinct character. Their feeling that they were a special breed of men, an exacting social and spiritual élite, a secret association of the elect, molded their whole inner attitude, their sense of fellowship, their supreme elegance.

That explains why so much of this poetry strikes us as far-fetched, strange, or hard to understand; even if we take the greatest pains in investigating the historical and philological origins of the conceptions prevailing among the courtly poets, we cannot penetrate to the essential content, the *dousa sabor* (sweet savor) that certain words and phrases possessed for them. Even today if we frequent a group of young men who profess to have devised their own new form of spiritual life, we find that among them certain words and constructions cast off their customary meanings and take on implications and tonalities that are well-nigh incomprehensible to the profane and utterly impossible to translate into everyday language. The analogy may help us to understand Provençal poetry, for in it blows a tenuous breath of subjectivist mysticism, difficult to interpret with our present knowledge. It may well have its source in the heterodox movements of the time, and in the case of Arnaut Daniel, for example, one is tempted to think of a secret language which conceals much more than erotic meanings. Be that as it may, it is certain that Provençal literature is not popular, universal, or accessible to all, but the possession of a particular circle, and that its ideas are those which were current in that circle. That aristocratic group possessed its own peculiar, though perhaps not conscious and systematic, notion of the form of the noble life. But since it was one of those cultural vanguards which discover the seeds of the future while those about them cling to old institutions and habits and often retain strength enough to impose their ideas, what the new movement created, as is always the case with a productive "fashion," is wholly situated in the realm of sensibility. To fashion it, to make it light and bold and elegant was their task and their accomplishment. Devoting all their freedom and vigor to "love," they transformed it so completely that it ceased to be anything more than a breath, an extract, of itself and was often little more than a pretext for a play of social and poetic concepts. For the Provençal poets love is essentially neither pleasure nor mad passion (although both these categories are represented) but the mystical goal of the noble life, and at the same time its fundamental condition and the source of inspiration.

Provençal poetry was brought to southern Italy by the court of Frederick II; as a foreign fashion, it also came to the towns of northern Italy and Tuscany, but there it did not find a receptive soil; the clumsy, pedantic love poetry written there at the time would have been forgotten long ago if not for scholars trying to track down Dante's predecessors.

A single man, Guido Guinizelli of Bologna, inaugurated the new style of Italian poetry and thereby created the first literary movement in the modern sense. Feudal society and customs had never flourished in Italy; no trace of a national culture has come down to us, and up to the beginning of the thirteenth century what literary works we find are crude, isolated, and for the most part of foreign origin.[1] The wars of the Hohenstauffen emperors and the powerful movement of the mendicant orders, chiefly the

Franciscans, drew Italy into the European medieval community, to which it had been a stranger for centuries; numerous writers, including myself, have called attention to the importance of St. Francis of Assisi for the renewal of imagination and sensibility in Europe,[2] and it is a fact that has long been known to art historians. That general rebirth of sensibility was reflected not only in religious experience but also in the political strivings of the Italian towns; it gave concreteness and individuality to the writings of the chroniclers and storytellers as well as to works of art. But the development was limited to the realm of sensibility. The great political and religious currents combated one another and disintegrated in the course of the thirteenth century. It was not from a great, universal movement that Dante drew his first inspiration but from the formal culture of a small circle which consciously adopted the Provençal tradition, all the more enthusiastically in view of its esoteric, foreign character. The social foundations of Provençal poetry were lacking in Italy, but that did not prevent Guinizelli, the founder of the Italian movement, from taking over the Provençal heritage of a highly stylized poetry expressing a select, aristocratic form of life, hostile to vulgar expression. For chivalric Provence he substituted the imaginary land of the *cor gentile*—and this very spiritual notion, which was a religious ethos but not the universal Church, a common homeland but no earthly country, was the foundation of the first independent artistic movement in modern Europe. It was the only bond that united the companions of the *dolce stil nuovo,* but it produced an intense feeling of fellowship among them and the heady atmosphere of a secret association of initiates and lovers. *Al cor gientil repadria sempre amore* (Love is ever present to the gentle heart) is something very different from Bernard de Ventadour's *Chantars no pot gaire valer* (Song cannot avail) or *Non es meravelha s'eu chan* (It is no wonder if I sing). The freedom and spontaneity of the Provençal poets, naïve with all their formal refinement, had given way to a creed, an ethos with its strict principles and strict obligations. Whereas Bernard had taken his culture of feeling and thought for granted, because his country and environment had instilled it in him along with his personal gifts, Guinizelli had to achieve this same culture by self-discipline, and it became all-important to him. For him the social bond that united the Provençal poets had vanished; the community of the *cor gentile* was an aristocracy based on a common spirit—a spirit which unmistakably encompassed certain secret conceptions and rules. Consequently the poetry is obscure; but in its obscurity, for which the poets of the older generation reproached Guinizelli,[3] there is far more consistency and coherent discipline than in the Provençal poets. A number of attempts have been made to interpret it, that is, to explain rationally and systematically what is unintelligible to us,[4] but in vain—all of them have been fanciful and forced. That, I believe, is not wholly explained by the prejudices and insufficient knowledge of their authors. It seems to me, rather, that the problem itself is insoluble, for an authentic occult doctrine is not a rational system that is concealed only for external reasons and might be divulged to all, but is something secret by nature, which is never fully known even to the initiate and ceases to be itself the moment one tries to make it universal. Yet the futility and frequent absurdity of these attempted explanations should not lead us to deny the obscurity of most of the poems of the *stil nuovo,* or to look for historical explanations in each single case: for that there are too many oddities, the correspondences in content and expression between different poets are too patent, and there is too much evidence of a secret meaning accessible only to the elect. Even the now prevailing opinion that the *stil nuovo* was a purely literary convention or fashion does not, I believe, strike at the core of the matter, though often "literary convention" is taken in so wide a sense that it comes close to the mark. Here and throughout the Middle Ages, the literary was not an autonomous concept as it became in the modern world. *Amore,* its source and principle, was religious in character. But the religious inspiration of the *stil nuovo* was not only mystical but also in high degree subjective. Its essential themes are: the power of love as a mediator of divine wisdom; direct communication between the mistress and the Kingdom of God; her power to confer faith, knowledge and inner renewal on the lover; and, finally, the explicit restriction of such gifts to lovers, coupled with the contemptuous vilification of all others, of the lowly vulgarians who understand nothing

27

and against whom lovers are warned to be on their guard. That conception, which recalls mystical, Neo-Platonic, and Averroistic currents, is at the very least a radical sublimation of the teachings of the Church; it is an independent doctrine which can still find a place within the Church, but borders very closely on heterodoxy. And indeed a few of the adepts were looked upon as free thinkers.

Guinizelli wrote between 1250 and 1275; the most important poets of his group were Guido Cavalcanti (c. 1250–1300), Dante Alighieri (1265–1321), and Cino da Pistoia (roughly the same age as Dante, died in 1337). In the circle of the *stil nuovo,* Dante did not at first represent a new frame of mind; Cavalcanti was more original in his thinking than he. In his subjection to the power of *Amore,* in his exaggerated esoteric sensibility, in his sustained style, he was a faithful follower of Guinizelli.

But from the very first day he was a new voice; a human voice so rich and strong that none of his contemporaries can reach his measure in suggestive power. There is no doubt, it seems to me, that he exerted this power even then, though only in the small circle of his youthful companions, whose minds were open to such things. In *Purgatorio* xiv, 21, Dante does not wish to mention his name to a man from Forlì, who had died some fifty years before, on the ground that he had no very wide renown at the time, so that the other can scarcely have heard of him. For it should be remembered that vernacular literature in the lofty style was something very new in those days and limited to a restricted circle. Other indications carry all the more weight. Cavalcanti, who was by birth, position, and intellect the leading light of the group, and who was considerably older and more influential than Dante, recognized him at once as his friend and companion, and his love and admiration are discernible even in the sonnet bitterly abjuring his old love for Dante (*Io vegno il giorno a te infinite volte* [Each day I come countless times to thee]).[5] Already in the *Vita nuova* we find references to the opinion of Dante held in this circle; for example, when a friend asks him to write about the nature of love, *avendo forse per l'udite parole* (Dante's canzone *Donne ch'avete*) *speranza de me oltre che degna*[6] (having perhaps, because of the words he had heard, set greater hope in me than I deserve); and the famous reference in *Convivio* i. III to the *molti che forsechè per alcuna fama in altra forma m'aveano imaginato*[7] (many who, perhaps because of something they had heard, had formed a different picture of me) can essentially refer only to his fame as a poet. In one of the first cantos of the *Inferno*[8] he has the great poets of antiquity welcome him as one of them—a device he would surely not have permitted himself had there been any danger that his reader would find it ridiculous. And the same applies to the transparent allusion in the speech of Oderisi da Gubbio.[9] This sense of his own worth and indeed Dante's whole attitude are those of a man whose first youthful efforts had delighted his contemporaries, who from the very beginning was regarded as a man apart by his companions of the *stil nuovo*. Still more eloquent of this attitude and of his success as a young man are the scenes in the *Divine Comedy* where the dead companions of his youth greet him with the most famous of his own verses: the enchanting encounters with Casella the musician[10] and with the young King Charles Martell[11] recall evenings in Florence when the canzoni in question were applauded for the first time by the youthful élite. Even Bonagiunta da Lucca, a poet of the older generation, who had looked with disapproval upon the *dolce stil nuovo,* welcomes him with the first of his great canzoni: Are you, he asks, he who wrote the verses in the New Style, beginning: *Donne ch'avete intelletto d'amore* (Ladies that have intelligence of love)?[12]

Let us try to form a somewhat clearer idea of the voice of Dante's youth by comparing his poems with those of his companions. We begin with the best known poem of the *Vita nuova,* the sonnet on his lady's salutation.[13] It runs:

Tanto gentile e tanto onesta pare
La donna mia quand'ella altrui saluta,
ch'ogne lingua deven tremando muta,
e li occhi no l'ardiscon di guardare.
Ella si va, sentendosi laudare,
benignamente d'umiltà vestuta;
e par che sia una cosa venuta
da cielo in terra a miracol mostrare.

29

Mostrasi si piacente a chi la mira,
che dà per li occhi una dolcezza al core,
che 'ntender no la può chi no la prova;
e par che de la sua labbia si mova
un spirito soave pien d'amore,
che va dicendo a l'anima: Sospira.

My lady looks so gentle and so pure
When yielding salutation by the way,
that the tongue trembles and has nought to say,
And the eyes, which fain would see, may not endure.
And still, amid the praise she hears secure,
She walks with humbleness for her array;
Seeming a creature sent from Heaven to stay
On earth, and show a miracle made sure.
She is so pleasant in the eyes of men
That through the sight the inmost heart doth gain
A sweetness which needs proof to know it by:
And from between her lips there seems to move
A soothing spirit that is full of love,
Saying for ever to the soul, "O sigh!"[14]

From the hand of Guido Guinizelli we have the same theme in two different forms. In the first he links it with the praise of the beloved in general:[15]

Voglio del ver la mia dona laudare
et asenbrargli la rosa e lo giglio.
come stella diana splende e pare,
e zo ch'è lasù bello a le' somiglio.
verde rivera me resenbla, l'aire
tutti coluri e flor, zano e vermeglio,
oro e azuro e riche zoi per dare.
medesmamente amor rafina meglio.
Passa per via adorna e si gentile
cha sbassa argoglio a cui dona salute
e fal de nostra fe se no la crede;
e non si po apresare homo ch'è vile.
ancor ve dico c'ha mazor vertute:
nul hom po mal pensar fin che la vede.

I would praise the sight of my lady
and liken her to the rose and the lily.
she shines resplendent as the morning star
and resembles all that is beautiful on high.
she reminds me of a green bank, of the air,
of all the colors and flowers, yellow and red,
gold and blue and rich jewels fit for a gift.
and all these are further refined by love.
She passes by the way, lovely and so gentle
That pride is spent in him to whom she gives greeting
and if he is not of our faith she converts him to it;
a man of base heart cannot approach her.
and I say to you, she has still greater virtue;
no man can think evil once he sees her.

The other sonnet describes the effect of the greeting on himself:

Lo vostro bel saluto e l gentil sguardo
che fate quando v'encontro m'ancide;
amor m'assale e già non è reguardo
s'elli face peccato over mercede.
che per mezzo lo chore me lanciò un dardo,
ched oltre 'n parte me talgla e divide,
parlar non posso, che 'n gran pene ardo,
si come quelli che sua morte vede.
Per li occhi passa come fa lo trono
che fere per la finestra della torre
e ciò che dentro trova spezza e fende.
remagno chomo statua d'ottono
ove vita ne spirito non richorre,
se non che la fighura d'omo rende.

Your fair greeting and the gentle glance
you cast when I meet you destroy me;
Love assails me and cares not
whether he does good or ill.
for through the middle of my heart he has shot an arrow
which pierces and divides it through and through,
I cannot speak, I am consumed with pain,
like one who sees his death.

31

He passes through my eyes like the lightning
that strikes through the window of the tower
shattering all it finds within.
I am left like a statue of bronze
to which life and breath will never return,
and which presents only the aspect of a man.

Finally, let us consider a sonnet on a similar theme by Cavalcanti:[16]

Chi è questa che ven ch'ogn' om la mira
e fa tremar di chiaritate l'a're,
e mena seco amor si che parlare
null' omo pote, ma ciascun sospira?
O Deo, che sembra quando li occhi gira
dica'l Amor, ch' i'no'l savria contare:
cotanto d'umiltà donna mi pare,
ch'ogn' altra ver di lei i'la chiam'ira.
Non si poria contar la sua piagenza,
ch'a lei s'inchina ogni gentil virtute,
e la beltate per sua dea la mostra.
Non fu si alta già la mente nostra
e non si pose in noi tanta salute,
che propriamente n'aviam canoscenza.

Who is she coming, whom all gaze upon,
Who makes the air all tremulous with light,
And at whose side is Love himself? that none
Dare speak, but each man's sighs are infinite.
Ah me! how she looks round from left to right,
Let Love discourse: I may not speak thereon,
Lady she seems of such high benison
As makes all others graceless in men's sight.
The honour which is hers cannot be said;
To whom are subject all things virtuous,
While all things beauteous own her deity.
Ne'er was the mind of man so nobly led
Nor yet was such redemption granted us
That we should ever know her perfectly.[17]

What first strikes us in considering these four poems[18] is that Dante confined himself to describing as vividly as possible the actual greeting and its immediate effects, while the two Guidos offer both more and less. The first of Guinizelli's sonnets begins with a declaration of intention: *voglio del ver la mia donna laudare.* Then comes a list of metaphors which do not seem to rise systematically to a climax but merely to be set side by side for their cumulative effect. The salutation is presented as a new theme which crowns the whole, but it is not seen as an event. Guinizelli seems interested only in bringing out its miraculous aspect, which he does very elegantly by listing its effects. But his statement is too precise, as though he were speaking of demonstrable facts; by the third line of this section, the eleventh of the sonnet, he has risen to such a pitch with the overemphatic line about the conversion that in the few remaining lines he is obliged to make two fresh beginnings. Thematically, Guinizelli's second poem has far more unity; but here again he is not interested in the event but only in its miraculous effect, which he again exhausts in the second line with the crass word *ancide;* the rest of the poem is a commentary on that word. The first tercet surprises us with the beautiful image of the storm, which continues to the end of the poem. It is one of the finest passages that has come down to us from Guinizelli; it clearly shows the nobility and authenticity of his feeling and also his concern for the concrete, but makes it equally clear that that same concern for the concrete has its source in allegory and analysis.

The younger Guido begins with a full tone, as though to thrust us into the midst of the event, and carries on in one breath through the fourth or perhaps the fifth line. But on closer scrutiny we see that the sensuous force of the image breaks off after the second line; for the metaphor of the trembling air, the statement that *ciascuno sospira* has no more to do with the perception of an actual event than does the harsh and purely intellectual antithesis of *umiltà* and *ira.* Very quickly he gives up trying to say what he cannot say, and the elegance of his apology cannot blind us to the fact that the tone of the first line promises more than the poem fulfills.

Dante's opening is much less dramatic than Cavalcanti's; he

33

seems to be speaking not of something present but of a memory —until the second clause of his comparative consecutive period draws him into the actual event with its gentle and insistent crescendo. Then he is in it, and there follows one of those rare passages that enable us to grasp and demonstrate what is utterly new in a poetic style: with the words *Ella si va* he resumes the theme, now treating it as present. With those words he creates the illusion of a continuous event, as it must have been in his mind: his lady appears and salutes, all fall silent and fear to look her in the face; then she is past but still in sight, some of those present venture a whisper, and only now does the first comparative image appear, springing quite naturally from the inspiration of the moment; and then, when she has passed from view, with the ninth line, memory begins, in lines of mounting intensity, to dwell on the vision and to savor it. Meditation on the vision culminates in a deep sigh, which ends it and breaks the spell.

Guinizelli's first sonnet is rich in themes. He was remarkably inventive, and nearly all the motifs and images of the *stil nuovo* go back to him. It was he who first ventured to make the lady, who in Provençal poetry remained, in principle at least, an earthly being, a mediatrix of the highest grace and knowledge, and created the framework of the new rhetorical apparatus which that transformation required. This rhetoric, based on an ethos, is perfected in a poem where the subject can be treated in entirely theoretical terms—the famous canzone on the place and nature of love (*Al cor gientil repadria sempre amore*).[19] Here Guinizelli repeatedly transposes a lofty thought into allegorical comparisons; the allegory suggests a new thought, and thus, through statement, demonstration, and transitional metaphor, he arrives at the enchanting final image, which in turn culminates in a *bel parlare,* an aphorism. Thus thought at once sensuous and sublime is captured in a network of pure and somewhat contradictory concepts.

But his cool intellectualism, which warms only when the meanings he is playing with take on the dignity of ethical categories (a method which Dante does not reject but which he carries into a broader context) detracts from his power. Perhaps his flight from the concrete event was a necessary consequence of the inner transformation he incurred in attempting to write in the lofty style in a land whose culture had not yet taken form, or perhaps the still crude Italian language, though already remarkably eloquent in the popular style, was, on the sublime level, better suited to states of mind than to events. That would be strange, for the contrary tends to be true in the history of language. However, there is no doubt that in twelfth-century Italy, the shift from sterile old age to youth was far more abrupt than in France or Germany; only a short time before the language of literature had been a senile Latin, and the literary vernacular had scarcely come into existence when the rhetoric of the *Volgare illustre* was born. In his poems written in the lofty style—others have come down to us—Guido Guinizelli was a philosophical, rhetorical poet and nothing else: he mentions an event only in order to analyze its effects. In the poem under discussion he lists four different ethical effects of his lady's salutation in five lines, but because the strict sonnet form prevents him from freely developing his allegories and spinning out his ideas, he merely piles statement on statement.

There is still another passage in the *Vita nuova* where Dante describes the ethical effects of his lady's glance. He tells how Love awakens at the sight of her (*Ne li occhi porta la mia donna Amore*[20] [In her eyes my lady bears Love]); Love's awakening is preceded by a process of inner purification which ascends from stage to stage, provoked by his lady's glance, her salutation, her words, her smile. We experience the course of events along with the fortunate man favored by so miraculous an encounter; and with his parallel repetitions and frequent recollections of the sensuous reality, Dante makes a delightful game of the antithesis between the seemingly tenuous cause and the profound effect, which in Guinizelli was still cold and dogmatic. Still, the sonnet as a whole is not one of the most successful; it is marred by the apostrophe in the middle (*aiutatemi donne* [help me, ladies]), a device which is usually very effective in Dante but which here, at the end of the quatrain, seems like a colorless interruption. Again, in the third stanza of his early canzone, *Donne ch'avete intelletto d'amore,* he invites the ladies to accompany his mistress if they wish to make a noble appearance, for at the sight of her the power of Love kills all base thoughts. Then Guinizelli's themes follow in an articulated crescendo. By his picture of almost unendurable effort and by means of a concrete disjunction that gives the image necessity and intensity, Dante transforms Guinizelli's abstract statement

> *e non si po apresare home ch'è vile*

into

> *e qual soffrisse di starle a vedere*
> *divverria nobil cosa, o si morria*

and he whom she suffered to gaze upon her
would become noble or else would die.

The formation of the two endings is quite parallel: but in Dante the end is really a climax in which the ethical effect shifts into an "anagogic" hope, while in Guinizelli it is only a statement which has quite accidentally turned up at the end and which gives us no sense of the promised augment.[21]

The great canzone of which we have been speaking is highly instructive in still another respect. We have spoken of the *spell* which at the end of the salutation sonnet reaches its climax and is broken with the word *sospira*. In addition to pleasing the hearer and gaining his approval, Dante strives, in nearly all his poems, to cast a spell upon him; and in the finest of his poems his tone gives the impression not of a communication but of an incantation, a summons to share his inner being, to follow him—and the power of that appeal is enhanced by the fact that it is addressed not to all but only to the elect. Consider such a line as:

> *Donne ch'avete intelletto d'amore . . .*

It is an apostrophe: but it is more. It is an appeal, a summons, expressive of a supreme demand and a profound trust. At one stroke the speaker has singled out the circle of the elect from the throng of the living and gathered them round him; there they stand, removed from all else, prepared to listen. The apostrophe is a favorite device with Dante; but we should not conceive of it as a mere technical trick, for it is a natural expression of his power and authority. The apostrophe in Europe was as old as lit-

erature: Homer used it frequently (we need only think of Chryses'
address to the Atrides at the beginning of the *Iliad,* which vividly
evokes the image of hands raised in supplication); and Demosthenes' οὐ μὰ τοὺς ἐν Μαραθῶνι (No, not by those who in Mara-
thon . . .), was remembered by all who were prepared to emu-
late the Greek tone. Christian prayer, hymns and sequences gave
new life to the apostrophe; but I believe one would search the
whole profane literature of the Middle Ages in vain for an apostrophe carrying so powerful a spell. Even the Provençal poets,
who sometimes employ apostrophe at the beginning and in the
tornada of their great canzoni, scarcely achieved it; to Guinizelli
it was quite unknown. It was reborn with Dante.

His first sonnet, *A ciascun' alma presa a gentile core* (To every captive soul and gentle heart), begins with an emphatic appeal to the elect of love; but what here is a light and graceful in-
vitation soon becomes supplication or summons.

*O voi che per la via d'Amor passate—Morte villana, di pietà
nemica—Piangete, amanti, poi che piange Amore—Donne
ch'avete intelletto d'amore—Voi che portate la sembianza umile—
Se'tu colui c'hai trattato sovente—Deh peregrini che pensosi an-
date* (O ye who pass by the way of Love—Vile death, enemy of
compassion—Weep, ye lovers, for Love is weeping—Ladies that
have intelligence of love—Ye of humble mien—Art thou he who
hath often spoken—O pilgrims who wander deep in thought):
these apostrophes contained in the first lines of the poems of the
Vita nuova show the unprecedented power of Dante's voice: the
magic they draw is that of the poet's inspiration and those caught
in its spell must follow him until he sets them free. This form of
direct address may also occur in the middle of a poem; and the
significance of the final word *sospira* in the salutation sonnet is
made evident to the most dispassionate observer by comparison
with the *ciascun sospira* in the sonnet of Cavalcanti reprinted
here. Or another example: in the dream recounted in the canzone
Donna pietosa e di novella etate[22] (Compassionate lady, young
in years), the evil omens take concrete form in the messenger
who addresses him directly:

> . . . *Che fai? non sai novella?*
> *Morta è la donna tua, ch'era sì bella* . . .

What are you doing? Don't you know the news?
Dead is your lady who was so fair . . .

Dante was given to apostrophe from the start and used it over
and over again with amazing diversity of tone. From the great
poems of his late period we may recall the lines:

Voi ch'intendendo il terzo ciel movete
udite il ragionar ch'è nel mio core . . .[23]

You who by your understanding move the third heaven,
hear the words that are in my heart . . .
or:

Amor che movi tua vertù dal cielo . . .[24]

Love, who derivest thy power from heaven . . .

As we have said, direct apostrophe occurs not only at the beginning, but often in the middle of a poem, as in the canzone *La
dispietata mente*[25] (The offended heart), in which the invoca-
tion is repeated over and over, or in the magnificent *Io son ve-
nuto al punto de la rota*[26] (I have come to the point on the circle), where the outburst he has long been leading up to is in the
end almost muffled: *Canzone, or che sarà di me . . .* (Canzone
what will become of me . . .). We should have to copy a hundred
lines or more from the *Divine Comedy* if we wished to give an
idea of its wealth of apostrophe. The list begins with the address
to Virgil: *Or se'tu quel Virgilio . . .* (Art thou that Virgil . . .)
and ends with the prayer to St. Bernard in the last canto or, if we
prefer, with the *o luce eterna* (O eternal light) of line 124. Urgent
command and gentle plea, afflicted prayer and confident appeal,
challenge to debate and friendly greeting, the joy of meeting an
old friend: all are represented in the long list; some of these apostrophes climax a long preparation and pour forth in several
mighty verses; others consist only in an interjection: *Deh. . . .*[27]

We have seen that in Dante's early poetry the concrete event
has replaced the rhetoric in which Guinizelli expressed his state
of mind and that Dante seems not merely to communicate but to
cast a magic spell. But they are not the only reasons for the
power of his voice. There is also something quite new in Dante's
sentence structure; for the present we cannot describe it in de-

tail but merely say that the thought is so articulated as to become melody. If side by side with the poems of the *stil nuovo* we read some of the famous Provençal songs, such as *Can vei la lauzeta* (When I see the lark) of Bernard de Ventadour[28] or Giraut's Alba,[29] or Peire Vidal's *Ab l'alen tir vas me l'aire*[30] (As I draw breath, the breeze), we cannot fail to see how little logic there is in the syntax of those works. We do occasionally find causal, consecutive, final, or comparative connections: but they do not dominate the whole; the cohesion is provided, rather by an almost indefinable something, by a vague, irrational lyric mood. The embodiments of mood, which form the various sections of the poem, are for the most part juxtaposed without any logical connection; in this respect the Provençal lays differ only slightly from popular poetry. Temporal organization predominates, while the logical connections, when not extremely simple, tend to become vague and obscure; the preference for the short line, particularly that of eight syllables, works in the same direction by creating a kind of hopping rhythm in contrast to the even flow made possible and indeed demanded by the predominance of the hendecasyllabic line, the *superbissimum carmen*.[31] Of course there are exceptions among the Provençal poets, particularly the later ones; or rather, the *trobar clus* shows a distinct striving for logical structure which, however, partly from intent and partly from incapacity, remains capricious, unclear, and uneven. Actually the pure lyricism of the earlier poets seems not only more harmonious, but also more rational than the *trobar clus* with its obscure intellectualism. In either case we seldom find a harmonious logical structure and a smoothly flowing period. There are rare exceptions such as these lines of Guilhem de Cabestanh:

> *Lo jorn qu'ie us vi, dompna, primeiramen,*
> *Quan a vos plac que us me laissetz vezer,*
> *Parti mon cor tot d'autre pessamen*
> *E foron ferm en vos tug mey voler*[32]

The day I first saw you, lady,
When it pleased you to let me see you,
My heart turned away from all other thoughts
And all my desires were gathered in you.

Here a simple motif is carried consistently through four hendeca-syllabic lines, and although the connection is purely temporal, the tone is almost un-Provençal, suggestive of the Italian *stil nuovo*.

From the very start, even in the Sicilians, or in Guittone or Bonagiunta, Italian poetry is far more logical and coherent in structure. The Italian poets soon gained a clearer grasp of their subject matter than the troubadours; they seldom give the impression that something has been left unclear or unsaid, and the periods, in contrast to those of the Provençal poets, seem sober and robust. Logical structure came naturally to Guinizelli, but with him it is sublimated and adapted to the ethos of the *cor gentile;* as we have already pointed out, his poems in the lofty style are not very concrete, but his concepts stand out all the more clearly; the unintelligibility that Bonagiunta criticizes in him is not so much, as in the *trobar clus,* the result of arbitrary, irregular connections, but springs rather from the novelty and unusual sublimation of the intellectual categories on which Guinizelli based the spirituality of the *stil nuovo.* The *tenson* in which he argues with Bonagiunta on the obscurity of his poetry[33] is highly instructive in this respect; Bonagiunta's opening (*Poi ch'avete mutata la manera* [Since you have altered the manner]) with its somewhat crude bonhomie, with its clearly articulated sentences that are in truth only one, with its antithesis and aphoristic summation, is a representative example of the early Italian clearheadedness that we find in the short stories and anecdotes; and Guinizelli's high-toned and meaningful reply (*Omo ch'è sagio non corre legero* [A wise man does not run lightly]) shows, with its rich logical organization, that self-discipline and higher spirituality have sharpened and by no means dulled his wits even for that sort of contest. If we consider a Provençal poem related in content, Giraut's *tenson* on the *trobar clus* (*Era m platz, Giraut de Borneill* [It was my pleasure, Giraut de Borneill]),[34] the difference in logical structure is quite clear; Giraut tries to keep his poem on a far more theoretical plane but does not succeed; the argumentation remains very general and vague, none of the ideas is taken firmly in hand, and the connections are uneven; at the end there is a startling digression and the dispute vanishes into thin air. When Guinizelli wrote in the lofty tone—that he could also do otherwise is shown by such poems as the sonnet *Chi vedesse a Lucia un var chapuço*[35] (Should you see Lucia in a bright-colored hood)—he links his ideas together and illustrates them by comparisons; where he has space to develop them, link is added to link with transparent clarity. The deep seriousness and the ethos of his inspiration save him from appearing pedantic; but there is still a certain stiffness and monotony in his syntax, a natural consequence of his purely intellectual approach to his themes. Often he is obliged to make a fresh start in the middle of a poem, because a new idea sets in which, though thematically connected with the last, seems completely new for lack of a poetic connection, and the whole gives the impression of a successive series. He himself felt the need for greater cohesion and concreteness, but the means he employs to this end—resumption of a word or sound, repetition of constructions and figures of speech, particularly comparison and antithesis—tend rather, in his long canzone *Al cor gentil,* where they are most in evidence, to increase the effect of dogmatic rigidity. He does achieve a pure linear harmony, but compared with Dante, it seems very thin.

In statement and structure Dante is no less clear and complete than his master; but what was the essential in Guinizelli is in Dante only an emanation of deeper forces. The structure of his poems is neither pre-intellectual like that of the troubadours nor purely intellectual like that of Guinizelli; it is something else. One reason for that, as we have pointed out, is that Dante's poems spring less from a feeling or an idea than from an event. But there is more to it than that, for Dante's events are seldom real or even conceivable in empirical terms; in the main they are visions. Consider the content of the final poem of the *Vita nuova: Oltre la spera* (Beyond the sphere). From the motif: my spirit often dwells with my dead beloved—a poet like Guinizelli would scarcely have made more than two lines; in order to write more, he would have had to move away from his point of departure, that is, from himself, and introduce something else, a related but new motif, perhaps a description of the condition of the departed, a message from her, in short an assortment of different elements. But when Dante's spirit wanders aloft, his vision of the event is all of a piece; there is nothing metaphoric about it; it

41

is as though he were registering a real event in slow motion; the whole poem is a record of his spirit's ascent and return. However —and this is what gives the poem its special poignancy—it is not the poet's whole spirit that sets out on its journey: a part of it remains waiting below, and only the *sospiro* to which Love lends an intelligence, rises upward and becomes *spirito*. The opening words and even the account of the spirit's sojourn above give us the feeling of someone staying behind and looking after the departed one as Noah may have looked after the departing dove or as we today follow a departing plane with our eyes and then with our thoughts long after it has disappeared from view. This parallel transposed into the heart of the event (and clearly stated at the end of the poem) sharpens and intensifies the unity of the poem, which is a well-articulated structure, governed by a single theme; the one theme is clearly set forth in the opening lines, and nothing "new" is added.

In all his early poems Dante is very sparing in the use of new, supplementary motifs; usually the main theme is so concretely individual that it suffers no additions and draws its intensity from its inner structure and the visionary sharpness with which it is depicted. But even where he deals with a very general theme, it is transformed by the keenness and range of his perception; it ceases to be a mere figment of thought and seems to become a concrete historical reality. An example of that is provided by the programmatic poem about *Amore* and the *cor gentile;*[36] in his long, treatise-like canzone, Guinizelli was able to weave the steps of his thought into a poetic whole only by the logical development of his metaphors. As it stands in the poem, the opening line (though it can easily be reinterpreted as a synthetic summary) is merely the first link in a chain; Dante's opening line is clearly the sum of the whole thought, and the birth of Love follows in a well-formed vision. The schema in which the poem seems to be cast is only apparent (Dante says so himself with the words *potenzia* and *atto*); for the second part is not an independent "addition"; it is neither logically nor thematically a new link, but a development and actualization of what was set forth in the first line; and for that reason the poem, despite its didactic tone, gives us a sense of looking on as a bud opens. The most universal

42

theme, which the poets of the *stil nuovo* treated again and again, is the praise of the poet's lady, and it cannot be denied that even Guinizelli, although he devised new themes and infused into them the new spirit of the "gentle heart," possesses far less concrete directness than the Minnesänger or the troubadours; for where the troubadours and Minnesänger achieve a free and perfectly lyrical outpouring of feeling, he merely piles up statements: (*Voglio del ver la mia dona laudare* or *Tengnol di foll'empres'a lo ver dire* [In truth it seems a mad venture]).[37] In the *Vita nuova* Dante treated this theme only once in its most general form, in the great canzone *Donne ch'avete;* everywhere else he preferred a particular motif or event, but here he explicitly announces his intention to speak in the most general terms: *io vo' con voi de la mia donna dire* (I will speak to you of my lady). For the moment we shall disregard the new element of urgency and personalization introduced by the words *con voi* and the confession in the third and fourth lines[38] (... not that I think I can exhaust her praises; I speak to relieve my mind); we have already attempted, in speaking of the apostrophe, to explain this "I with you," and here we wish only to call the reader's attention to the inner forces Dante is able to release by the use of this rhetorical form. At present we are concerned with the general structure of the poem: it is not perfect, for Dante did not succeed in doing what he was able to do later in dealing with very general themes, namely to avoid a juxtaposition of diverse images. But even so, the poem is something very different from Guinizelli; for though as a whole it is "pieced together" and certain lines of the fourth sonnet, the praise of the "gentle" body, are a mosaic of metaphors, nevertheless the pieces that Dante fits into the mosaic in the course of his thematic development—the scene in heaven, her appearance in the street, Love who beholds her— are a sequence of visions emanating from a central vision. These visions do not seem wholly alive to us, and some of the images seem forced; but even the manner in which they are forced is new: instead of a capricious *trobar clus* or of Guinizelli's elaborate intellectualism, we have a real power, for Dante's whole striving is to intensify his feeling to the utmost by raising it above the sphere of subjectivity to which feeling is ordinarily confined, to give it objective validity by establishing it in the empyrean realm of the ultimate and absolute. That is his sole concern, and that endeavor is reflected in the immoderate metaphors and contrasts which outdo even the mystical rhetoric of the *stil nuovo*. Even today we feel the power of this will, and the poem with all its unevenness still breathes the same magic. It is the magic exerted by Dante's passion for unity, by his striving to involve the whole cosmos in his own experience. The direction of his feeling is so definite that it cannot be deflected by the awkward rational order of the poem but operates, in the parts and in the whole, as a radiation of power, as a fiery enchantment.

Thus the unity of Dante's early poetry, which is still more evident in other poems with more concrete and more sharply defined themes, is not of a rational but of a visionary character; the images of which the poems consist are not conjured up by a listing of characteristics but arise complete and real, from an essential center, and that is how they operate; they are alive with radiant forces; they desire power and they gain it. Everywhere Dante speaks from the center of a very definite, unmistakably unique situation; everywhere he wishes to drive the listener into this situation; sympathy or approval, not to speak of intellectual admiration, is not enough for him; he insists on being followed into the extreme particularity of the real situation that he conjures up. It would be inaccurate and perhaps unjust to say that his experience was stronger and more immediate than that of the earlier poets of the Middle Ages; and there is in his verses a considerable element of strain and exaggeration, which springs not from the prevailing taste but from his desire to express himself at any price. The truth is rather that the earlier poets tend to branch outward from their experience, to adduce, through association or logical connections, everything that is in any way related to the experience or likely to explain or ornament it metaphorically, whereas Dante holds firmly to his concrete point of departure and excludes everything else, whether alien, related, or similar. He never spreads himself thin but digs down. The surroundings and attendant circumstances vanish as he digs, often with painful concentration, deeper and deeper into his concrete motif. His metaphors are highly characteristic in this respect. In the *Vita nuova* they seldom have an independent poetic value as in the Provençal poets or Guinizelli; they never lead to a new territory, they provide no new image or relief from tension: they are often brief and scant, but always close to the event. Their purpose is neither poetic pleasure nor intellectual clarification nor a combination of the two; they are pure expression, and they make their appearance where they are useful for expression. Consequently the composition of most of the poems has a cohesion and unity that may have seemed both bare and pedantic to the older generation. Seldom does one of the customary poetic ornaments appear; and when it does, it is not introduced with taste and charm, but is so immoderately exaggerated, so earnestly transposed into the realm of reality as to frighten and repel Dante's older contemporaries. By its insistence on the concrete, unique situation, by its unabashed disclosure of personal feeling the poem takes on such an intensity that those who were not prepared to commit themselves with passion felt wounded and alarmed.

The style of Dante's early poetry is both stricter and richer than that of his predecessors: It is stricter in the sense that a definite theme is adhered to from start to finish of a poem. That method, which gives an effect of realism and immediacy even when the most daring and unusual themes are treated, was nothing new. It had long been known, though not in the lofty style; comical, pastoral, or polemical subjects had often been treated in this way; there was a natural inclination toward it in Italy, and we have already mentioned two poems, one by Bonagiunta (*Poi ch'avete mutata la manera*) and one by Guinizelli (*Chi vedesse*) in which it is employed with a certain mastery. But before Dante's time that procedure had not been adopted in lofty vernacular poetry, because poetry of that kind was held to be fundamentally artificial, unrealistic, rhetorical—a very old conception which Dante threw off only very gradually and never with conscious consistency. What makes Dante's style richer than its forerunners is that he delves more and more deeply into his theme and organizes it from within. This makes for a more natural style, better adapted to the manifold aspects of the reality he is treating.

These elements, which are hard to keep apart and tend to

merge in the course of any analysis—Dante's closeness to his theme, his tone of conjuration, the visionary unity of his composition—account by and large for the novelty of his style and showed Europe the possibility of a new tone in sublime poetry. From his predecessors he took the mystique of the *cor gentile,* the poetic forms of the canzone, sonnet, ballade, and indeed the whole terminology of the rhetoric of love—but from all this he made something entirely new, and ultimately, despite his paroxystic flights of feelings, despite his concentration on extraordinary experiences accessible only to the few, something far simpler. We need only read his sentences as prose: *Tanto gentile e tanto onesta pare la donna mia, quando ella altrui saluta, ch'ogni lingua deven tremando muta e li occhi no l'ardiscon di guardare* (My lady looks so gentle and so pure when she greets others that the tongue trembles and falls silent and the eyes dare not look upon her). Or: *E perchè me ricorda ch'io parlai de la mia donna, mentre che vivia, donne gentili, volontier con vui, non voi parlare altrui, se non a cor gentil che in donna sia*[39] (And because I remember that while my lady lived I gladly spoke of her with you, I wish to speak of her to none other than to the gentle heart that dwells in ladies). This is clear and simple, and moreover the lines flow even when we look at them and still more when we hear them. This was beyond Guinizelli. Because he heaped up ideas, he had to keep making fresh starts; repeatedly the stream of feeling is blocked; he takes a new breath, and after a few words it stops again (to observe this we need only to read one of his poems after reading Dante). With all their transparent simplicity, Dante's poems have a powerful rhythm, an unbroken natural movement from within, that had not been witnessed since antiquity. The impression we are describing here, still more than the other aspects we have mentioned, is purely sensuous, because its motivations were still wholly unconscious and involuntary. However, if we distrust the baffling simplicity of the lines, we can find out a little more about it. *Ne li occhi porta la mia donna Amore, per che si fa gentil ciò qu'ella mira*[40] (In her eyes my lady bears Love, wherefore all she looks upon is ennobled). Could anything be more clear and simple? An almost didactic causal nexus, two members of equal weight, each word firmly and clearly in its place—apart from *ne li occhi* there is nothing in the sentence that could not be prose. But what content! In it the lofty feeling, the noblest conceptions of the *cor gentile* are presupposed and taken for granted; it is as though he took the summit as his starting point and there found a new plane on which to move; and in each one of these clear simple words vibrates a world of spiritual ennoblement. That becomes still more evident when we consider sentences that are somewhat more complex. *Donne . . . i'vo'con voi de la mia donna dire, non perch'io creda sua laude finire, ma ragionar per isfogar la mente. Io dico che pensando il suo valore, Amor si dolce mi si fa sentire, che s'io allora non perdessi ardire, farei parlando innamorar la gente* (Ladies, I will speak with you of my lady, not because I think to exhaust her praises but in order to relieve my mind. I say that as I think of her worth, Love speaks to me so sweetly that if I did not lose courage I should make everyone fall in love by my words). Like those above, these sentences seem to contain quiet, carefully formed statements, and the seeming moderation of the logical, highly prosaic sentence structure is further enhanced by the even flow of the syllables and the way in which they are worked into the rhyme scheme. But now let us consider the content of such sentences. They deal not with facts and ideas but with storms of passionate feeling, which seem here to fall with the greatest ease into a strict syntactic and metrical form. *Can vei la lauzeta mover de joi sas alas contra l rai, que s'oblid 'e se laissa chazer per la doussor c'al cor li vai, Ai! tan grans enveya m'en ve de cui qu'eu veya jauzion . . .* (When I see the lark in a transport of joy flying into the sun, losing consciousness and falling lifeless, his heart smitten with an excess of delight, alas, great envy invades me of those whom I see so full of contentment . . .). This too is a long flowing period; but how much more freely and simply the passion pours forth. Even the second generation of Provençal poets had forgotten, or consciously turned away from, this "singing as the birds sing"; it was replaced by an effort to capture feeling in thought, a tendency we discern very early, but most clearly in Giraut de Bornelh and Arnaut Daniel. The dialectic of feeling—that term seems to me closest to the reality[41]—consists in forming a logical or seemingly logical system (sometimes concealing an occult wisdom) from words signifying the feeling, its origin, psychological setting and effects. Attempts at a dogmatics of love are old; they were inspired by the example of Ovid and by the vulgar spiritualist tendency to subordinate sensuous reality to a rational interpretation; the most famous example is the book of Andreas Capellanus. But the form owes its first truly poetic treatment to the later Provençal poets who raised conflicting ideas to such a pitch of intensity as to suggest a tragic struggle. But the strange and often highly suggestive poems they wrote in that way are based on a conscious aesthetic conception, a conscious striving for something extraordinary, paradoxical, and difficult to understand; that is already evident in the technique of contrasts, a form so unrealistic and abstract that it often obscures the actual occasion of the poem. In general the generation which strove once again to discipline the free lyrical flow in more set forms, favored a purely formal development of conceptual relations and intricate rhymes at the expense, not of feeling, which remained the substance of their poems, but of the reality of the underlying experience. Thus their rationality is spurious, capricious and fantastic; their purpose is not to give form to a concrete reality but to devise a game of contrasts and obscure metaphors. That poetry shows a certain kinship with the logical and rhetorical games of vulgar spiritualism and can perhaps in the last analysis be traced back to the degenerate rhetorical tradition of late antiquity. Dante's dialectic of feeling is something very different. Quite unconsciously at first, it harks back to the authentic sources of ancient rhetoric, that is, to the Greeks. For although Dante did not know Greek, though he had only the vaguest notion of Homer and none at all of the tragic poets—although he had drawn his classical culture from a few Latin authors who seem, from our point of view, to have been selected quite arbitrarily—none the less he is the authentic heir of what is noblest in ancient Greece, of the "language that created μὲν and δὲ";[42] his sentences are the first since antiquity which contain a world and are simple as the lines of a primer, which express deep feeling with the clarity of thought, which pierce the heart with their quiet even measure; above all they are the first in which rhetoric does not suppress reality but forms it and holds it fast.

Dante himself dealt theoretically with these matters. In the sixth chapter of the second book of his *De vulgari eloquentia* (Of Writing in the Vernacular) he speaks of *constructio* or sentence structure. The passage that interests us most runs: "What we seem to be looking for is the congruent construction. But no less difficulty is involved in the investigation we must undertake before we can arrive at the construction we are seeking, namely that which is most urbane. For there are many degrees of constructions: the uncouth that is used by those without learning, for example: *Petrus amat multum dominam Bertam.* (Peter dearly loves his wife Bertha.) Then there is the purely learned that is employed by strict scholars and schoolmasters, for example: *Piget me, cunctis pietate maiorem, quicunque in exilio tabescentes patriam tantum sompniando revisunt.* (I, who outdo all others in compassion, am filled with regret for those who, languishing in exile, will never see their homeland again except in dreams.) There is the learned and elegant style of those who draw superficially on rhetoric, for example: *Laudabilis discretio marchionis Estensis et sua magnificentia preparata cunctis illum facit esse dilectum.* (The laudable discernment of the Marquis of Este and his generosity to all make him well beloved.) There is also a style that is learned and elegant and at the same time lofty, employed by the illustrious stylists, for example: *Eiecta maxima parte florum de sinu tuo, Florentia, nequicquam Trinacriam Totila secundus adivit.* (After he had shorn thy robe of the greater part of its flowers, O Florence, the second Totila [Charles of Valois] went in vain to Trinacria [Sicily].) This degree of construction is the one we call the most excellent, and, as we have said above, it is the one we seek when we deal with the highest things. This is the construction used in the noblest canzoni, as for example that of Giraut, *Si per mon Sobretots non fos.* . . . (If it were not for my Only Friend. . . .) (Here there follow more examples, all drawn from Provençal and Italian canzoni; then he continues): Reader, do not be surprised that I call so many authors to mind. For only by such examples can we indicate what we call the highest construction. And perhaps it would

49

be most useful, by way of accustoming ourselves to it, to read the well-constructed poets, such as Virgil, the Ovid of the Metamorphoses, Statius, and Lucan; as well as the authors who have written the most excellent prose, such as Livy, Pliny, Frontinus, Paulus Orosius, and many others whom friendly solitude invites us to read. Let then the devotees of ignorance cease to extol Guittone d'Arezzo and certain others who have never ceased to be plebeian both in words and construction."[43]

Eduard Norden[44] cites this passage and not without reason judges the stylistic examples very severely. Naturalness and simplicity are condemned, he says, while unnatural bombast is justified. However, we gain a somewhat different view if we consider that in writing this passage Dante was not thinking of Latin prose but of vernacular poetry in the lofty style, and that accordingly these sentences are presented not as models of Italian prose but rather as analogies by which to elucidate his ideas on style in Italian poetry. Thus we should not consider the four sentences by themselves but in this general context; we can appreciate their true significance only if we keep in mind vernacular poetry and particularly the Provençal and Italian canzoni cited in the same passage.

One is struck at once by the fact that Dante adduces four degrees of style, whereas the traditional χαρακτῆρες λέξεως are three—Dante himself in several other passages, in the fourth chapter of the same book for example, speaks of a threefold classification. But actually, in the present passage, he distinguishes only two types of sentence structure, the vulgar type, *genus humile,* of the first example, which is rejected, and the lofty style of which he cites three variants: the first learned and pedantic, the second superficially elegant, and the third learned, elegant, and lofty in one. All three aim at richly articulated expression and loftiness of tone. The first tries to achieve that end with explanatory antitheses which are injected, by a number of rather laborious syntactic artifices, into the simple statement: I feel sorry for exiles; the sentence is overloaded and sounds stiff. The second sentence is smoother and more urbane, but it lacks power and body; it is one-sided, without counterweight, and sounds empty. In the third, which Dante favors, our modern taste is disturbed by the pun on Florentia, by the circumlocution *Totila secundus,* and in general by the spurious language employed. But undeniably the sentence has a ring to it when read aloud. It should not be taken as a prose sentence but as a poetic analogy; it expresses an antithesis which finds a close parallel in the ingenious construction, consisting of two almost equal periods, one rising and one falling, separated by the apostrophe Florentia. And despite all the ornamentation the content—namely, he despoiled thee, Florence, but went in vain to Sicily—is set forth in striking clarity.

Dante's intention becomes still clearer when we consider the canzoni that he cites as examples of true loftiness. They all belong to the stylistic trend that we identify with the "dialectic of feeling." Perhaps Vossler has something similar in mind when in speaking of this passage he stresses the classical element in the poetry quoted.[45] However, the antithesis of classical and romantic, which Vossler employs here, though to be sure with prudent restrictions, strikes me as inappropriate to the thirteenth and fourteenth centuries; it is not quite accurate and allows of misunderstandings. The dialectic of feeling that is the new element in that poetry is far more romantic than classical in inspiration, and with the exception of Dante, none of the poets possessed what I should call the classical element in it. Dante was delighted with the *excellentissimus gradus constructionis* that he found in these canzoni; Vossler calls them "show pieces" and contrasts them with those "which affect us not so much by their art as by their spirit and above all by the natural freshness and simplicity of their language."[46] These are the poets of direct feeling and almost purely pre-intellectual composition, who "sing as the birds sing" and whom Dante scorns to mention. It is certain that Giraut de Bornelh, Folquet de Marseille, Arnaut Daniel, and the other poets mentioned by Dante no longer sang with the same spontaneity and overflowing feeling as Jaufre Rudel and Bernard de Ventadour,[47] and that they wrestled with a great difficulty; but their poems are far from being mere show pieces, nor are these obscure verses with their intricate rhymes mere art for art's sake. Like almost all the mannerist works of medieval art—and the same still applies to the true mannerism of the sixteenth century—they embody a spiritualism of Neo-Platonic origin, a strongly subjective mysticism which reinterprets and sublimates sensuous appearance in order to attain the idea but at the same time seeks to preserve the unique, particular appearance. None of these poets succeeded; the expansive drive with which they sought to encompass the depths of the soul and the glittering breadth of the outside world was doomed to frustration. Their metaphors miss the mark, become hollow and blurred; their ideas, instead of clinging to the subject, remain vague and abstract, capricious and fanciful; they strive for inner unity of structure but more often than not what unity they achieve is purely artistic and external. There is something tragic about them all, and particularly about the poet whom Dante admired most, the *miglior fabbro del parlar materno*[48] (the best craftsman of his mother tongue), Arnaut Daniel. He was a man of extraordinary talent and possessed the same mysterious mixture of passionate sensuality and strict, logical thinking as Dante. He was, though he himself benefited little by it, the first poet who designedly heightened his expressiveness by the use of commonplace or even grotesque images, and with his hard, impetuous, and often almost hysterical temperament sometimes achieved antithetical formulations of intense passion which, by way of Dante and Petrarch, were to influence all European poetry. Of this the poem quoted by Dante contains a number of examples, and there is genius in such lines as these:

> *Anc ieu non l'aic, mas ella m'a*
> *Totz temps en son poder....*[49]

> Never have I her, it is she
> Who has me always in her power. . . .

But he is seldom able to sustain his tone. His thought fights his passion and refuses to keep pace with it; the reader must look for ingeniously hidden meanings and the total effect is lost. However, we must not interpret as capricious ornament what was ethos and necessity. His thought struggles to grasp the sensuous reality and falls back time and time again into the void, into a game of concepts. It is a drama of more than aesthetic interest, for the way from thought to reality leads through poetry. Here in any case lay the beginning of a significant development, and that too I believe is of more than aesthetic interest.

And so Dante admired in these poems their *excellentissimus gradus constructionis,* their richness of articulation and their high-toned dialectic of feeling. He failed to see what distinguished him from his masters, and perhaps he never became clearly aware of it. Or should we find an indication to the contrary in the sentence *et fortassis utilissimum foret:* "And perhaps it would be most useful, by way of accustoming ourselves to it [the noble construction], if we should read the Latin poets. . . ." It is certainly our best way of ascertaining what Dante contributed that was new in this respect. Of course the novelty is not to be sought in his remarks about the influence of the ancients. Earlier poets had also read the classics. For Dante, as for the earlier poets, the primary factor was an inward striving for form, and such a striving was already present in high degree when he found both a confirmation and a model in the poems of Virgil and the other Latin writers. But he did revive the rhetorical poetics of antiquity more penetratingly and fully than anyone before him, though his methods of course are entirely different from those of the ancient poets.

In the Provençal poets regularity of composition was based on versification and rhyme; they possessed a cultivated feeling for words, they loved games with words and rhymes; but the characteristic ancient foundation of the lofty style, the art of the period, was relatively alien to them. To be sure, the Provençal poets of the second style made frequent use of a few rhetorical forms following from their penchant for antithesis; we recall, for example, how Giraut de Bornelh in his famous canzone of antitheses (*Un sonet fatz malvatz e bo*[50] [A sonnet ill made but beautiful]) employs a kind of sentence-parallelism supported by the regular caesura after the fourth syllable—a rather monotonous and primitive device, it will be admitted. Arnaut is richer and more daring, but the center of his formal endeavor is to be sought in his art of rhyming, and even though Canello, who edited his works, rightly praises the absence of padding and patchwork in his poetry,[51] his sentence structure is definitely weakened by his tendency to choose words and sounds for their striking effect. There are plenty of eloquent passages, but nowhere—even less than in Giraut—do we find a free continuous flow, a clear delimitation of the different parts of a construction.

Dante wonderfully combines the art of rhyming with regularity and sharpness of sentence structure. In *Al cor gentil,* Guinizelli, guided by similar considerations, tries in each stanza to give equal place and equal rhythm to statement and metaphorical explanation, but the effect is thin and schematic. In the same medium Dante achieves freedom of movement; even in the restricted space of a sonnet he moves with perfect ease and fluency. It is scarcely necessary to remark on the natural regularity of such a poem as the sonnet *Tanto gentile;* any fairly attentive reader will notice that the end of each period coincides with a metric section, that the end of each line with its rhyme is the conclusion of a phrase or, if not, that the part lifted out of it (*la donna mia*) is systematically and meaningfully set apart, and above all that lines which correspond in metric position and rhyme also reveal a parallelism of meaning and syntax. And all this does not give an effect of artificiality but seems to flow naturally from the subject matter. Perhaps the best way to show how Dante clarified the period will be to quote a few rather complicated sentences from a canzone which Dante himself cites as an example of the lofty style. It is one of Arnaut's best-constructed poems. The second stanza runs:[52]

> *D'autras vezer sui secs e d'auzir sortz*
> *Qu'en sola lieis vei et aug et esgar;*
> *E jes d'aisso noill sui fals plazentiers*
> *Que mais la vol non ditz la bocal cors;*
> *Qu'eu no vau tant chams, vauz ni plans ni puois*
> *Qu'en un sol cors trob aissi bos aips totz:*
> *Qu'en lieis los volc Dieus triar et assire.*

I am blind to the charms of other women, I am deaf to their voices. It is to her alone that I give heed, for her alone that I have eyes and ears. And this is no vain flattery: my heart desires her still more ardently than my mouth bears witness. I may pass through hills and dales, through fields and plains: in a single being I continue to find all the virtues. God selected them for my lady and established them in her.

It is evident that from the third line on the connections are negligent and unclear in meaning; the same conjunction is used over and over, but not always in the same sense; the distinction between dependent and independent clauses is blurred, and in general the syntax is without plan or order. Now let us look at a poem by Guinizelli:[53]

> *Da llei non ò sembiante,*
> *ed ella non mi fa vist' amorosa:*
> *Perch'eo divengn' amante*
> *se non per dricta força di valore*
> *che la rende giojosa;*
> *onde mi piace morir per su'amore.*

> She looks not upon me
> With eyes of love:
> And so I fall enamored
> Solely by the force of her worth
> Which makes her radiant:
> Wherefore I would die for love of her.

Here everything is perfectly clear and plain; but have we a period? No more and no less than in Arnaut; in meaning, yes, at least up to the penultimate line, but, syntactically no; the structure is cumulative, a concealed parataxis. And now a sentence from Dante's own canzone:[54]

> *E certo e'mi convien lasciare in pria,*
> *s'io vo' trattar di quel ch'odo di lei,*
> *ciò che lo mio intelletto non comprende;*
> *e di quel che s'intende*
> *gran parte, perchè dirlo non savrei.*

> And surely, if I wish to speak of what I hear of her, it behoves me to set aside what my mind does not understand—and a large part of what it does understand, because I should not know how to say it.

Little comment is necessary: no sentence of that kind was written in the Middle Ages before Dante, although we have finer periods from his hand. Let us merely consider that by placing *ciò* at the center of the whole construction and giving almost

55

equal accent to *gran parte,* Dante has achieved a perfectly satisfactory substitute for the Greek μέν and δέ. However, this canzone
is not strictly speaking a work of Dante's earlier years. Since our
main aim here is to show that Dante was a new voice from the
very first, we must go back for a moment to the *Vita nuova.* It
is not as though he favored complicated hypotactic periods in
these early works; he had learned a number of things from the
schools of rhetoric, the *artes dictandi,* but that influence did not
become very pronounced until later, in the *Convivio* and the late
canzoni, and he was never inclined to a strict subordination of
clauses. Each clause preserves its independence; often the clauses
are coordinated, and not infrequently a new construction sets in
abruptly with the result that a clause seems to be torn out of its
period. For the most part the sentences are simple, and their
structure is evident at a glance. But as we have said, that simplicity must be viewed with suspicion; it is the product of a long
process of formal purification, of the stylistic strivings of several
generations. *E qual è stata la mia vita, poscia que la mia donna
andò nel secol novo, lingua non è che dicer lo sapesse.* (And what
my life has been since my lady departed to the other world, no
tongue can say)—that simple sentence expresses fact and feeling
in one; its only rhetorical artifice consists in two syntactical an-
ticipations of the main statement. But a sentence of that kind
required the flowering of an ethos of love that would make its
meaning seem natural to the reader; it required a language, and
in the thirteenth century Italian was still a Latin vernacular; and
it required Dante's genius. For none of Dante's companions of
the *stil nuovo* was capable of expressing an emotion with such
simplicity. When Guido Cavalcanti, the most important of them,
wrote in the sublime vein, he was never able to cast off the artistic
methods of the late troubadours. The stylistic examples cited in
the section of the *De vulgari eloquentia* to which we have referred
include a *ballata* by him:[55]

> *Poi che di doglia cor conven ch'i'porti,*
> *e senta di piacere ardente foco,*
> *e di virtù mi traggo a si vil loco,*
> *dirò com'ò perduto ogni valore.*

E dico chi i miei spiriti son morti
e'l cor ch'a tanta guerra e vita poco;
e se non fosse che'l morir m'e gioco
fare'ne di pieta pianger amore.

Ma per lo folle tempo che m'a giunto,
mi cangio di mia ferma oppinione
in altrui condizione
si, ch'io non mostro quanto sento affanno
la'nd'io ricevo inganno;
chè dentro de lo cor mi passa amanza
che se ne porta tutta mia possanza.

Because it beseems my heart to grieve
and yet I feel ardent pleasure,
and from virtue I descend to place so vile,
I will tell you how I have lost all worth.
I will say how my spirit is dead
and my heart as well that has suffered so much strife;
and were it not that to die is nothing to me,
I should make love weep with pity at my lot.

But in the days of folly that have come upon me,
I alter my condition
By resolute design
So that I show not what grief I feel,
Wherefore I suffer injury,
for love inhabits my heart
And destroys all my strength.

If Dante cites this short poem along with a number of long canzoni, as an example of the sublime style, we may be justified in supposing that it was his favorite among his former friend's works. What must have moved him in such verses is the note of passionate confession, the daring sharpness of the word order, the almost arrogant brevity and obscurity of the antitheses. But beneath the arrogance is hidden not only an erratic nervousness but also a kind of impotence inherited from the *trobar clus,* which in Petrarch's hands was to become the basis of a radically subjective literary tradition. These lines are purely personal, the poet dwells with a kind of monomania on his inner situation;

there is not the slightest fragment of configured reality, and the cause of the poet's mood is indicated only in the most general and obscure terms. The syntactical connections are clear, though by no means as sharp as in Dante; the force of the poem is not in its general structure but in its antithetical words and statements. Exactly as in the *trobar clus,* the formative impulse is limited to a subjective interpretive play with concepts, which creates a strange atmosphere and discloses the soul of the speaker. But in this subjective medium Cavalcanti has a far surer touch than Arnaut, partly because in the meanwhile the *stil nuovo* had built up a system of concepts and metaphors better adapted to extreme subjectivity than was the language of the Provençal love song, and partly because Cavalcanti with his bold, complex mind anticipated a form of culture that was not to flower until much later: Lorenzo de' Medici's admiration for him is very revealing. However, Cavalcanti's genius, like the *trobar clus,* was wholly grounded in the vulgar spiritualist rhetoric of concepts and was in no way affected by the glimmer of true antiquity, to which Dante owed his feeling for sensuous reality and his art of sentence structure. In the *Divine Comedy,* Dante's former friend is contrasted with Virgil in a passage that has been variously interpreted:[56] *Forse cui Guido vostro ebbe a disdegno* (Whom perhaps your Guido held in disdain). The meaning, I believe, is not fundamentally aesthetic; the dialogue with Cavalcanti's father makes it clear that Dante is speaking here not of Virgil the poet but of the reason-inspired guide sent by Beatrice. However, the two are hard to separate. For Dante, Virgil, as master of the sublime style, was the supreme embodiment of reason—a poetic reason which took hold of reality and transformed it into vision. From this antique reason alone he learned the sublime style which was the foundation of his fame—it gave him what his predecessors and contemporaries could not give him.

Let us once again sum up what we have said about Dante's early writing. It embodies no essentially new ideas or attitudes; but in it we hear a new voice of unprecedented fullness and power. We have noted, more or less at random, a few of the traits that make up Dante's style: He is concerned with real happening and records it with penetrating vividness; he does not communicate, but adjures and challenges; through limitation and inner articulation, he gives unity and flow to the thought structure, the dialectic of feeling that he has taken over from the Provençal poets and Guinizelli; and lastly we noted that his way of organizing his material is closely bound up with a feeling for clear and regular sentence structure, derived from the study of ancient authors. Now we may attempt to classify those traits, to establish what they have in common, and to discover their sources in Dante's personality.

We observe at once that the last two considerations—organization of content and sentence structure—are merely two forms of the same thing, namely the striving for articulated unity. Thus we may speak of three hallmarks of Dante's style. They are reality, adjuration, unity. They can be classified in two ways. Either we can start from the inner perception and say that its extraordinary intensity creates not only the realism but also the unity, since living perception always apprehends an articulated unity and not disjunct parts. Or conversely, we can start from the striving for unity; for the more powerful and passionate that striving is, the more irresistibly it will be driven to the concrete individual thing, which alone can give it satisfaction and fulfillment. In both cases the middle characteristic, the conjuration, becomes a mere measure of intensity, and in both cases it is clear that all three characteristics are expressions of the same force, seen in different aspects. That force is the unity of the person; its name is Dante, and in order to throw light on its genesis and development we must turn to the biographical information that has come down to us.

His family had long been resident in Florence, but it cannot, when Dante was a young man, have been particularly wealthy or esteemed. His mother seems to have died when he was a child, and certain obscure allusions in the *tenson* between Dante and Forese Donati[57] suggest that his father lived ingloriously and died unhappy. However, numerous passages in Dante's work and the reports of others show that he enjoyed an excellent and well-rounded education and that he had taken a part befitting his rank in the social, political, and military events of his youth. His marriage and the names of his friends confirm what we know from his early poems, namely, that he was at home in the leading circles of the nobility and upper bourgeoisie. Yet he probably owed that position more to his personal charm and talent than to his lineage and social standing, and that would account for its apparent ups and downs, for esteem due to personal accomplishments is far more dependent on caprice and fashion than is an inherited prestige. However, I do not believe that any very drastic conclusions should be drawn from the indications of his social vicissitudes (contained, for example, in his sonnet renouncing Cavalcanti or in his poetic controversy with Forese), nor does it strike me as likely that Dante was ever seriously poor before his exile; the sum of his debts shortly before 1300 suggests rather that his credit was good, and the tone in which he laments the poverty and uncertainty of his existence in exile makes it seem quite certain that he had not previously known such straits.

The crucial experience of his youth, the basic fact of his life, was the event which he himself described as his *vita nuova*—the story of his love for Beatrice. For our investigation it is a matter of indifference who Beatrice was and whether she ever existed; the Beatrice of the *Vita nuova* and the *Divine Comedy* is a creation of Dante and has little to do with the Florentine girl who later married Simone de' Bardi. Even if she is an allegorical figure standing for mystical wisdom, she embodies so much personal reality that we have a right to regard her as a human being, regardless of whether or not the real events described relate to any definite person. The notion of a simple alternative—either Beatrice really lived and Dante really loved her, then the *vita nuova* treats of a real experience, or else the whole thing is an allegory, consequently a deception, a mechanical fiction, and one of our finest ideals is shattered—any such notion is both naïve and unpoetic. All the poets of the *stil nuovo* possessed a mystical beloved; all of them had roughly the same fantastic amorous adventures; the gifts which Love bestowed upon them all (or denied them) have more in common with illumination than with sensual pleasure; and all of them belonged to a kind of secret brotherhood which molded their inner lives and perhaps their outward lives as well—but only one of them, Dante, was able to describe those esoteric happenings in such a way as to make us accept them as authentic reality even where the motivations and allusions are quite baffling. That in itself bears witness to the poetic genius of their author, and it is hard to understand why so many critics regard an erotic experience accessible to all as a better source of inspiration than a mystical illumination carrying the force of reality, as though poetic mimesis had to be a copy of appearances and did not distil its reality from the infinite treasure of images stored up in memory.

Thus the *Vita nuova* is useless as a source of information about Dante's actual biography; the events that occur in it, the meetings, journeys, and conversations cannot have taken place as they are here set forth and no biographical data can be derived from them. But the work throws an essential light on Dante's inner life. It shows how he derived the whole structure of his thinking from the love mysticism of the *stil nuovo,* and it indicates Dante's place among his literary associates. For in that early work we already find a creative logic, a gift of organization all his own, which enabled him to weave the equivocal abstractions of the *stil nuovo* into a unified whole. Despite all its eccentricities and the misunderstandings they create, that work left its readers with a very definite and undoubtedly justified impression: the impression of a visionary experience in which Perfection appears as a sensuous reality, courted by the poet, eluding him, and finally separated from him forever, though the separation bears the hope and promise of a true reunion. We find much that is strange, in particular the secondary characters, the *donna dello schermo* (screen lady), the dead girl, and the figures introduced toward the end; but even if we grasp their meaning dimly or not at all—and who can claim to understand them fully?—the work as a whole is not impaired, for these puzzling figures and events take on a sensuous, irrational reality which, even unexplained, finds acceptance in the imagination. And, as in no other writer of the *stil nuovo,* the center of the vision, a God-sent mystical wisdom, takes on so vivid and concrete a reality that even without supposing her to have been modelled on any living Florentine woman, we quite naturally join Dante in calling her Beatrice.

In Beatrice the oriental Christian motif of incarnate divine perfection, the *parousia* of the Idea, took a turn which has profoundly influenced all European literature. With his passionate, exacting temperament and his unflagging desire for a concrete embodiment of the truth Dante could only accept a visionary experience capable of legitimation by reason and act; he removed the secret truth, which in this case coincided with the first sweet enchantment of the senses, from the hazy private world of his companions and gave it a foundation in reality; his yearning for the truth did not turn to sterile heterodoxy or shapeless mysticism. In Dante the esoteric lady of the *stil nuovo* stands forth clearly for all to see; she becomes a necessary part of the plan of salvation, decreed by Divine Providence. The blessed Beatrice, identified with theological wisdom, is the necessary mediatrix between salvation and man in need of enlightenment, and it is only to the Romantic unbeliever of the nineteenth century that this seems pedantic or unpoetic; for Dante, the Thomist, to whom knowledge and faith were one, the sybilline beloved, empowered by Mary to save him by gradually revealing the truth—the true ideas and the true reality—was not a hybrid construction, but a living synthesis of sensuous and rational perfection.

Various motifs of different origin are interwoven in this myth of incarnate perfection. Beatrice is at once a Christian saint and an ancient sybil. As earthly beloved, she is a young man's dream, her contours barely discernible; transfigured, as a member of the heavenly hierarchy, she becomes a real being. What is original in this conception may not, at first sight, strike us as Christian; the troubadours had already introduced Christian themes into love poetry; earthly suffering and withdrawal from the world, ordinarily characteristic of a saint, seem to be lacking in the figure of Beatrice, while the didactic element, the revelation of a secret truth, suggests the syncretism of late antiquity and is not properly Christian. But the new element in Dante's Beatrice, what distinguishes her on the one hand from the lady of the troubadours and on the other from the ancient myths and the allegories of late antiquity, is something eminently Christian, more profoundly so than the troubadours' cult of the saints: she is transfigured and transformed while preserving her earthly form. The sybil is a supernatural being, she was never anything else; the lady of the troubadours is supernatural only in a meta-

phorical sense, the mythical gods who came down to earth sometimes travelled incognito, but their divinity remained intact, un-
affected by the world of men; they remained gods. Only Christ
was both one and the other: he was a man and transformed
himself; for the believer he transforms himself each day anew.

The earthly life and human suffering of Beatrice are barely
touched upon; yet they are present: we sense the fragrance of her
earthly person, which was young and admirably beautiful, felt
pain, and died; we witness her transfiguration and in it her
earthly form, her contingency, is preserved and enhanced. Consequently the *Vita nuova* is not, as some maintain today, merely
an uneven early work, unworthy to be considered independently.
Undeniably it is obscure in places, and undeniably its style is
hyperbolic; but the need for such hyperbole lay in the Christian
nature of the subject, in Dante's conscious synthesis of Perfection
with earthly frailty and uncertainty; obscurities springing from
this source may be found in every truly Christian mimetic creation, and most of all in the books of the New Testament. The
Vita nuova is in reality the necessary preliminary stage of Dante's
concept of reality, its very germ, and a necessary prologue to the
Divine Comedy. For Dante became what he was and is, the
Christian poet of an earthly reality preserved in transcendence,
in a perfection decreed by divine judgment, through the experience of his youth, and the *Vita nuova* is the record of this
experience.

To the very end his active life in the world was prefigured by
his youth. In the passionate, poetic experience of his youth, blood,
education, knowledge, political and philosophical tendencies were
fused and imbued with his personality, and the unity thus
achieved was poetic. Dante's whole life was poetic and his whole
person was that of a poet. Not in the Stoic-Epicurean sense, and
not of course in the Romantic sense of withdrawal from the
world, of an existence spent in abstract thought, contemplation,
or dreams. The man on whom Beatrice bestowed the magical
gift of her salutation had an inner authority, an expansiveness
that enabled him to weave the most personal aspects of his life
into a universal context and indeed, through his personal destiny,
to give new form to the universal order of the world, the great

serene drama of the Christian cosmos. His life with all its acts and strivings was poetic, because for him a poetic vision was the source and justification of action and practical reason, and because vision was his aim. In Dante the ethos of the *cor gentile,* originally an obscure, esoteric, and unreal form of thought, burst its limits, became concrete and universal. An attempt has been made to characterize the *Comedy* as a continuation of the Provençal *sirventes;* according to that reasoning the *sirventes,* in its limited sphere, was the negative, polemic aspect of a constructive life-form, while the censorious parts of the *Comedy* are merely a negative expression of a world-forming vision, whose roots lie hidden in the love poetry of Dante's youth, in his conception of the New Style. Dante was too resolute a man to content himself for long with a literary esotericism which barred off poetic dream life from the empirical life of every day: he came to regard the vision of Perfection that had been granted him as the true measure of human affairs, and he had the unbending strength of will to apply that measure, in the most practical sense, to the whole of life.

His unsuccessful political activity can only be regarded as an expression of this endeavor. The sacred measure of perfect beauty and order, which he had known and experienced, was the motivation of his political practice no less than of his political theory. That alone provides a satisfactory explanation of his political career, concerning whose beginnings and motivations no clear information has come down to us. In Florence an important process of social change had just been completed: the shift of power from the feudal nobility to the great financial and commercial bourgeoisie; but the general historical picture is obscured by the personal and family feuds, by the power politics that dominated the city's foreign relations, and by certain catchwords that were still in use though they had already lost all meaning; caste divisions had become fluid, a man's party allegiance was no longer determined by his origins, but by intrigues, economic opportunism, connections, and inclinations; the number of political protagonists was out of all proportion to the population. On the whole we have a picture of a young democracy undergoing its first crisis: unleashed greed and lust for power have begun to take possession of the state; chance business relations, unpredictable street brawls, constantly shifting alliances with neighboring cities make for a state of political uncertainty; no one is sure of his life and property; the protagonists change from one moment to the next, while in the background a few very shrewd and unscrupulous men, supported by the representatives of foreign political interests, lay the foundations of a great economic power that will later become a political power as well. The crux of the whole situation was the disintegration of the ideological world order. Crossed by other tendencies, the idea of a binding, all-encompassing order, a universal Christian peace in the arms of the Pope and the Emperor, had never been fulfilled in Italy and now, unable to withstand the many inner and outward upheavals of the day, it had even lost its function as a desire common to all men; the idea survived the *trecento* only in odd subjective forms; by 1300 it had lost its significance for the political life of the towns. Vast individual powers were unleashed, which sometimes operated together and sometimes at cross purposes; relations with the Pope and Emperor, which formerly had supplied at least an ideological foundation of the earthly order, ceased to be anything more than counters in a game, to be moved about as the situation demanded. With the defeats of the Hohenstauffen and the interregnum, the Empire had lost all its power in Italy; and the Pope was the intractable Boniface VIII, of whom good and bad can be said, a man rich in virtues and vices, who in any event was not the one thing that his position demanded, namely the representative of a divine institution. That might be explained by the inadequacy of human nature, which can never be fully equal to such a position; but Boniface did not even wish to be. With all his talents he was a formless, chaotic individual, dominated by practical interests and lust for power. His actions were not so much evil in a Christian sense as simply un-Christian. He was all earthly passion, devoid of any inner direction or striving, a visible symptom of the crisis in Christian political ideology. That man was Dante's adversary; he wished to exploit the chaotic situation of the Tuscan cities in order to dominate them; victorious only in appearance and for a short time, he was soon engulfed in the chaos he himself had summoned up. But in the meanwhile Dante, defeated, had outgrown the opportunism which had at least played a part in his first political acts; he had no desire to benefit by the fall of his adversary, for the new victors were just as alien and odious to him.

Dante has often been represented as a reactionary medieval politician who failed to understand the new social forms that were in the making, as a dreamer and dogmatist who defended the rigid forms of an obsolete ideology against the living forces of history. That view is perfectly defensible, but I believe that those who hold it misplace the accent because they are caught in the prejudices of this age which has one-sidedly developed the ideas of evolution and immanence at the expense of the static and transcendent elements in political and historical thinking. Dante was not an impractical ideologist; growing up in Florence, he was early trained in practical political activity; he served on city-planning commissions; he lived in a highly commercial society, and the princes who granted him their hospitality during his exile valued and made use of his diplomatic skill. Thus if, after an unsuccessful attempt to make his way in the existing movements and parties, he remained almost totally isolated, if his hopes betrayed him and he spent the last years of his life as an impoverished exile without political influence, it was not because he lacked ability to recognize living forces and participate in them, but because he had to reject those forces. For him the concepts of "history" and "development" would have had no validity in themselves; he asked for a sign by which to interpret events and he found only chaos; on every hand individuals advanced illegitimate aspirations and the result was confusion and disaster. For him the measure of history was not history, but a divine and perfect order of the world: a static, transcendent principle, to be sure, but this does not mean that it was abstract and dead. In his youth he had beheld divine perfection; to him it was a concrete experience, the sensuous embodiment of a lifelong yearning. We shall speak of that later on in greater detail; here I wish only to insist that since Dante was the most universal thinker of his day, unequalled in his knowledge of men, it is not permissible to explain his political misfortunes on the basis of childish mistakes and misunderstandings; he was unsuccessful and unhappy because his character and his fate did not permit him to be successful and happy; not because he failed to understand the rise of the city-states, or because he did not properly estimate political trends in general (a theory put forward by a present-day historian who musters in retrospect a number of factors of which no one could have been aware in Dante's time), but because the development of the city-states seemed to him unimportant if not unfortunate, and because his political thinking was above calculations of personal advantage. If he made a mistake, it was his failure to become a *parte per se stesso,* a party for himself,[58] sooner than he did; it was the opportunism which led him, before his exile and for a short time thereafter, to accept whatever allies he could find in his struggle with the Pope, even though he unquestionably believed the Cerchieschi, the Whites, to be just as evil as their adversaries, only pettier and more cowardly.

Not only did Beatrice shape his life; she also gave him the voice which reflects his vision of a static, well-ordered perfection; we hesitate to employ the much abused word "classical," because the new, measured style, hostile to all formal extravagance, embodies an element of urgent unrest which is far removed from ancient art and poetry; a yearning for transcendence and transfiguration. In many men of his time, that yearning was so overpowering as to destroy their perception of the world; the spirit became utterly absorbed in mystical devotion to the transcendent figuration of its hope. Dante's intense feeling for earthly existence, his consciousness of power made that evasion impossible for him. He had seen the figure of perfection on earth; she had blessed him and filled him and enchanted him with her superabundant grace: in that decisive case he had beheld a vision of the unity of earthly manifestation and eternal archetype; from that time on he could never contemplate an historical reality without an intimation of perfection and of how far the reality was removed from it; nor, conversely, could he conceive of a divine world order without embracing in the eternal system all manner of phenomenal realities, however diverse and changing. Already in the poem of Beatrice, of her life, death, and transfiguration, the concrete reality is preserved with an intensity hitherto

67

unknown. In all Provençal poetry, as we have seen, there is a wide gulf between the poetic world and the real world; when there is a reference to the real world, it seems to stand all by itself, unrelated to the main content of the poem. In Dante, that gulf has vanished; each poem is an authentic event, directly set forth in its unique, contingent, and ephemeral this-worldliness; from personal experience it expands into the universal, whence by a kind of counteraction it derives its articulated form to become an immutable vision of reality in general, earthly particularity held fast in the mirror of a timeless eye.

Thus the way in which Dante's style grew out of the crucial experience of his youth can best be illustrated by the image of the seed that falls on ready soil. The mysticism of the *stil nuovo* was the soil whence grew his work—like the innumerable lyrical and didactic creations of the other devotees of *Amore*. But in the others the esoteric subjectivism became more and more exaggerated; after 1300 Guinizelli lost his purity and Cavalcanti his expressive lyricism, and the circle disintegrated; the mystical love lyrics of those poets degenerated into abstract didacticism and lost their radiance. Dante, however, preserved his vision and formed the Christian cosmos in its image. His heart was too big for an esotericism that locked itself up in secrecy; enduring within him, the experience of his youth underwent a transformation, expanding to encompass the immanent earthly world and pressing beyond it; it lent his voice fullness and tone, it showed him the way to the innermost core of earthly realities where their *character indelibilis* is preserved, and it enabled him to perceive in imperfect, mobile, changing appearances a perfect unity which he looked upon as a pledge and copy of eternal unity. At the highest summit of his vision the roots are still discernible; through the loved one, departed and transfigured, the mysticism of the *stil nuovo* dominates his great poem of the cosmos; through all the universality in the thought and feeling of that poem, we perceive a suggestion of youthful pride, of lofty aloofness, of "slender charm or cool dignity," which reminds one of the Provençal poets and of Dante's youth in Florence.

III

THE SUBJECT OF THE *COMEDY*

The expansive drive which the poetry of the New Style developed in Dante carried him out beyond the sphere of feeling and mystical experience; when he entered upon the second period of life, the *giovinezza,* or young manhood, which he himself in the *Convivio*[1] describes as the summit of our life, his vitality and inner sense of measure had so matured that, almost simultaneously it would seem, he turned to public life and philosophical doctrines, combining the two and beginning to shape them to his cast of mind. In that striving of his, the great tradition of a unified world view, made up of corresponding orders of knowledge, was preserved intact; that was the striving for universal concordance which A. Dempf has aptly called the foundation of the *Summa,* the dominant form of medieval philosophy.[2]

Before Dante wrote his great canzoni and the *Convivio,* the world of the *stil nuovo* had been a world apart. Sprung from the chivalric ideal, refined and spiritualized in Provence, cut off from its social roots by Guinizelli, it had still been restricted to the adherents of a particular sensuous and mystical culture; the criterion of nobility and aristocratic origin, although explicitly combated by Guinizelli, had seemed well-nigh inseparable from that artificial style with its obscure terminology and metaphors. Increasingly rational elements related in structure to the didactic philosophy of the time had made their way into that poetry; more and more, the fundamental conception of love as a noble discipline had taken on an ethical character, suggesting a mystical doctrine of salvation; essentially, however, the *stil nuovo* had remained esoteric, an aristocratic game of the passions; and it still bore only a vague, private relation to practical political life or to scholastic philosophy.

As far as politics is concerned, a number of writers have claimed, some of them quite recently, that the obscure metaphors and allusions of certain poems conceal a Ghibelline hostility to the Church, and that the whole fellowship of the *stil nuovo* pursued secret political aims. So far that thesis remains unproved, and in any event the political activity of the group was intermittent and negligible; though beyond a doubt the learned scholastics looked upon the New Style as something outlandish and suspect. It was Dante who undertook to fuse the whole world with the experience of his youth and order it according to the measures of that experience.

Before we go further, an introductory remark is necessary. We shall describe the path that led Dante to the *Comedy* as an unbroken development, a mounting fulfilment of his powers. The description seems to be contradicted by a crucial passage in the *Comedy,* the thirtieth and thirty-first cantos of the *Purgatorio,* where he accuses himself, before Beatrice, of grave error from which he has been saved only by the miracle of grace. But as to the nature of the error, which must have involved the very core of his being since it forms the starting point of the great poem, we have only the most general notion. All we know is that there was a falling away from Beatrice, a misdirected love, a striving for illusory treasures. Neither the biographical clues at our disposal nor the works that can be situated with some degree of certainty between the last poems of the *Vita nuova* and the generally accepted date of his journey to the Other World, give us any exact idea. In any case the philosophical view reflected in these canzoni and the political aims pursued by Dante at the time do not conflict with the spirit of the *Comedy;* on the contrary they are developed in the great poem and confirmed in all essential points; and purely carnal transgressions, unless they went hand in hand with a corruption of his whole being, could not have justified Beatrice's reproaches and Dante's confession in that passage. Accordingly, the best we can do is to accept Dante's error as a fact, even though we cannot discover its traces in

Dante's life and work. To deny it and abandon its literal reality in favor of an allegorical or soteriological meaning strikes me as without justification. It seems very likely that for a time Dante doubted the Christian verities and inclined toward a radical Averroism or a free-thinking sensualism; to discuss the passages in his work that might fit in with such conjectures would take us too far from our subject; they do not provide clarity.

Be that as it may, he himself stated clearly and precisely what is essential for our discussion. In the twelfth chapter of the second book of the *Convivio* he tells us how, seeking consolation after the death of his beloved, he began to read Boethius and Cicero's *Laelius;* how it had been hard for him to understand them; how, when he began to understand, he had been delighted to find in them confirmation of what he had already seen as though in a dream and set forth in the *Vita nuova;* how he now began to attend the schools and *disputationes,* where philosophy was really taught, and in the brief period of some thirty months had delved into philosophy so deeply that love for it expelled every other thought from his heart; and how he had set out to praise philosophy in the canzone: *Voi che'ntendendo il terzo ciel movete.*[3] That passage describes and interprets the beginning of Dante's philosophical development. His philosophizing sprang from a heartfelt need; in philosophy he found confirmation of what he had long suspected; in it his striving for universal unity found nourishment, and he began at once to shape a perfect synthesis of his own personal experience with his newly acquired knowledge. Thus the question of whether Dante was an original philosopher is poorly formulated. He was original in the same sense as most scholastic thinkers, whose significance resides less in any freeborn thought than in their striving for a systematic synthesis of different bodies of traditional thought. Just as Thomas Aquinas sought to combine Aristotelianism with the Christian Platonism of Augustine, so Dante tried to reconcile the Thomist system with the mystical ideology of the *cor gentile.*

Only a poet could effect a concordance of that kind. For the Thomistic doctrine is rational and even in philosophical matters hostile to intuitionism; the love mysticism of the *stil nuovo* was sensuous and poetic in origin and culminated in ecstatic revelation. At the start Dante's only means of giving poetic form to philosophical doctrines or of framing sensuous mysticism in terms of doctrine, consisted in the kind of re-interpretation that vulgar spiritualism had been carrying on for centuries; and consequently for him as for his companion poets, Amore became the rational appetite (*appetitus rationalis*) for wisdom or philosophy, while spiritual strivings became the *substantiae separatae,* that is to say, the angels of Thomist metaphysics. But with him the result was not the barren, abstruse didacticism to which allegorical re-interpretation had hitherto led, even in Guido Cavalcanti. Even if the reader scarcely understands their philosophical content, the philosophical poems—for example, the canzoni *Voi che'ntendendo il terzo ciel movete* (You who by your understanding move the third heaven), *Amor che ne la mente mi ragiona* (Love who speaks to me in my mind), *Amor che movi tua vertù dal cielo* (Love who bringest thy power from heaven)—are among the most enchanting of all his works. That Dante himself knew:

> *Canzone, io credo che saranno radi*
> *color che tua ragion intendan bene,*
> *tanto la parli faticosa e forte.*
> *Onde, se per ventura elli addivene*
> *che tu dinanzi da persone vadi*
> *che non ti paian d'essa ben accorte,*
> *allor ti priego che ti riconforte,*
> *dicendo lor, diletta mia novella;*
> *"Ponete mente almen com'io son bella!"*[4]

Canzone, I think there will be few
who wholly understand your thought,
so strong and arduous is your utterance of it.
Therefore if by chance it happen
that you should meet with persons
who seem not to have seized it fully,
I pray you to take comfort,
my cherished poem, and to say:
"Consider at least how beautiful I am!"

In these poems a fusion of philosophy and poetry was achieved for the first time; each of the two had attained a stage of perfection, where it was prepared to accept help from the other and was indeed needful of such help. It is no mere love of paradox which leads us to say that after St. Thomas scholastic philosophy was in need of poetry. Ordering reason reaches a certain end point (there are several other instances of that in the history of ideas, though none so striking as the present one) when it is no longer able to express itself, to perfect and resolve itself, except through poetry. The Thomist system of Being, with its soaring speculative hierarchy, rests on a foundation of strict self-discipline and sharpest rationality and implies a passionate striving for order closely related to the attitude of the *stil nuovo,* though to be sure only as Dante embodied it. The striving for order is the common element. But although St. Thomas is able without the concrete inspiration of the poets, to build the Aristotelian, Catholic world in a well-rounded system, an edifice in which God, the "separate substances," man, his soul, and nature all have an appropriate place, he does not people it with individuals named and separately characterized. Dante, on the other hand, lives amid the figures of his poetic fantasy, each one of which has sprung from the irrational inspiration of a concrete moment, and with the help of philosophical thought he is able to define the nature, place, rank, and activity proper to each figure. That, it seems to me, is what makes possible the fusion of poetry and philosophy which marks the style of Dante's canzoni (I am referring primarily to those canzoni which appear to have been written between the *Vita nuova* and Dante's exile[5]). Though transposed into rational allegory, the personal content is not lost, but is preserved as a foundation. The reader can take in both meanings together, for the poet, appearing as a man with his human experience, serves as a connecting link between them. The purity of the philosophical meaning is not impaired if, for example, we conceive of the intelligences of the third heaven, invoked by Dante, as a materialized band of sublime and radiant spirits, without exactly remembering what philosophical concepts are meant; for in injecting himself, as a man torn by conflict, driven by love toward a decision, as the soul whose fate is to be decided, into his abstract speculation, he gives his intellectual edifice an historical character; the historical figure is self-sufficient even if

73

our knowledge of the philosophy is incomplete. How essential the personal participation of the poet is to the charm of the philosophical poems can be judged from those canzoni in which, forsaken by Amore, he says nothing of himself and his own emotions; the impression we have described is absent. These poems —for example, *Poscia ch'Amor del tutto m'ha lasciato* (Since Love has forsaken me entirely) or *Le dolci rime d'amor ch'i'solia* (The sweet rhymes of love which formerly)—are little more than difficult and purely didactic argumentations which seem to justify the modern preference for prose treatment of such matters. But the canzoni in which Dante treats philosophically of his own fate can awaken no such impression in anyone with the slightest feeling for poetry. Where philosophical man, with his imperfection as demonstrated and formulated by St. Thomas,[6] with the contingency of his natural and acquired character, confronts the hierarchy of intellectual concepts and entities, there rises within him a poignant yearning for self-realization and self-perfection; it is quite legitimate to represent that striving in sensuous images, because only through them can the personal drama be made clear; the images do not mean "something else," they are the language in which the inner event is uttered and their meaning is one and identical with it. Thus the canzoni embody a system of correspondences, of parallel developments that are one, though they are treated separately in the commentary. The artful and meticulous composition of the poems is probably unequalled in the whole of literature. Dante's images never carry him beyond what he has set out to say, nor does passion ever make his expression turgid or imprecise. His intention and his genius both lead him to strive for an exact concordance: between expression and its object, between sensuous image and rational meaning, between one part and another, between the whole and the person of the prospective reader. It is in that spirit that he handles his lines, his stanzas, and his rhymes. The art of making his meaning, so full of deep thought and tenderness, flow naturally into complicated verse forms achieves its highest perfection in the canzoni; in his treatment of complex metrical structures he follows the example of Arnaut and the tradition of the *stil nuovo,* but he outdoes them all in natural harmony, in concordance between subject matter and the verse form in which it is couched.

The other, political aspect of his expansive drive, came to an end with the catastrophe of 1302, when Dante was exiled and soon thereafter broke, perhaps not entirely of his own free will, with the White party and its Ghibelline allies. With that rupture and the isolation which followed, the outward course of his life was set. From that time on he had no means of exerting political influence; he had lost not only his country, but also his party, which despite the defeats it had suffered remained a power and would have enabled him to play a part. It was then that he became the lonely and helpless exile, whose social and material position depended on the hospitality of his personal friends and patrons; and his strong sense of his own worth, his haughty bearing, inadaptability, and impatience with the trivia of everyday life added to the bitterness of his lot. He himself in the *Comedy,* in the prophecies of Brunetto Latini and of Cacciaguida, relates what befell him and what he suffered; and in the beginning of the *Convivio,* in the third chapter of the first treatise, he tells us that his unfortunate situation was one of his main reasons for framing the work in that form. Literary endeavor had become his only hope of satisfying the yearning for fame; he wished to achieve an authoritative position, to correct the poor opinion of him that his wretched situation might arouse. But intellectual authority demanded a coherent view of the world, which in those days meant an encyclopedic system; and to Dante it was self-evident that an exposition of his system involved a purifying meditation on his fate, a justification of his life and way of thinking. Such were the motives from which sprang the *Convivio* and in a profounder sense the *Comedy.* Both were planned as universal encyclopedias, as the sum of their creator's lifework.

In both cases Dante chose a new, hitherto unknown form—yes, that is also true of the *Convivio,* even though it is a commentary. Latin commentaries on the Scriptures, on Aristotle, on Peter Lombard's *Sententiae* were recognized as frameworks for philosophical instruction; but a work of encyclopedic philosophy in the form of an Italian commentary on his own Italian poems dealing with his own emotions, that was a project of almost presumptuous boldness, and the apology which takes up the whole first treatise is far from being a mere rhetorical exercise. However, its careful deductions and circumlocutions do not conceal Dante's proud confidence in himself and his work; in support of his contention that it is permissible to speak of oneself when it becomes necessary to purge oneself of infamy or when one's life offers a source of edification for others, he invokes Boethius and the *Confessions* of St. Augustine;[7] and his extensive, only seemingly humble apology for the vernacular as well as his attempt to justify the perhaps excessive difficulty of his exposition, carry a proud awareness that he Dante, and he alone, has rendered the mother tongue capable of being used in that way. Indeed, the achievement of Dante is most evident in the prose work. The canzoni might perhaps be compared with similar works of Guinizelli and Cavalcanti; the style of the *Convivio* was unquestionably newborn.

Here for the first time he cast off the stylistic peculiarities of the time to such a degree that the European voice which is his voice, rings out and becomes plainly audible. Those who, because of its didactic content, disparage the *Convivio* as a work of art, are not likely to form a clear idea of Dante's intention and genius; for Dante, and here I mean also the author of the *Comedy,* the goal of art and the highest conceivable beauty reside in the order of Being; the road to it leads through knowledge, which describes and demonstrates the unity of order, which is itself the supreme knowledge; thus for him beauty is not distinct from truth, and we have no ground for considering ourselves superior to such a view; it is far more reliable, more concrete and coherent than any modern theories on the philosophy of art, and at most we may be justified in regretting that so perfect a unity of reason and perception can no longer (or perhaps not yet) have any validity for us.[8]

Nor should it seem strange that we speak of a European voice in connection with an early Italian work. Dante says explicitly that he does not write for the learned who have striven only for money and public prestige and turned literature into a harlot; he writes Italian because he does not wish to serve learned Italians or foreigners who know Latin, but the unlearned in Italy who are capable of noble aspirations and greatly in need of lofty instruction.[9]

Here for the first time an appeal was made to the public which was to be the mainstay of the new European culture; from then on the basic works to which European cultural life owed its development were written in the various vernacular languages, for the public that Dante had in mind; they draw the vitality of their expression from the writer's native tongue, whatever it may be, but they all have one thing in common, the conception of a *volgare illustre,* or a noble vernacular: a literary idiom which maintains a constant give and take with the language of everyday usage and so makes the living element in thought and tradition, the part that is really worth knowing, available to all who are eager to receive it. That common conception, which started with Dante, is a unity in diversity, the true modern European Κοινή, or common tongue. Though it seems hardly possible to define the spirit of the "noble vernacular," perhaps we may give a general idea by saying that the new idiom embodies a striving for knowledge as a way to mastery of the world, for knowledge as a universally human act and destiny.

The language of the *Convivio* is almost devoid of the sensuous force which Italian prose already possessed at the time and which Dante himself commanded; here his only aim is rational clarity. We have noted similar qualities in his early poetry; the regular, balanced structure of the periods, the correspondence between the syntactical position of the component clauses and the logical value of their content, the clarity and precision of the causal, final, or consecutive connections; but in the *Convivio* those instruments, employed for their true purpose—didactic prose—set their stamp on the style; his systematic study of scholastic philosophy had shown Dante the logical richness of language, and now, for the first time in a Romance vernacular, he attained what has ever since been regarded as the specific quality of Romance languages: purity of logical structure, clear articulation. Even personal or polemical passion must be fitted to the mould and must never be allowed to express itself in a lyrical outburst incompatible with a didactic treatise.

The *Convivio* was never finished and no one has ever succeeded in reconstructing Dante's plan. Apart from the introduction, which may be regarded as the first treatise, there were to be fourteen more, each one commenting on a canzone; three of them were completed. The first, on the canzone *Voi che'ntendendo,* deals with the victory of philosophical endeavor over the mystical attitude of his youth, represented by the thought of his dead beloved; the second, on the canzone, *Amor che ne la mente,* praises the divine nature and purifying power of philosophy; the third, on the canzone *Le dolci rime d'amor* (The sweet rhymes of love) contains a discusion of *gentilezza,* the supreme value of the *stil nuovo,* here taken as an aspect of Thomist-Aristotelian ethics; *gentilezza* is defined as a gift of God to the soul that is in a perfect body, and it is through that gift that the virtues unfold. Since the virtues lead to happiness, the entire definition runs: *seme di felicitade messo da Dio ne l'anima ben posta*[10] (seed of happiness planted by God in the well-placed soul); here the ideal of chivalric love poetry attains its highest degree of universality, combining an ancient with a modern ideal. From Dante's remarks we know that the fourteenth treatise, or thirteenth commentary, was to be devoted to the poem *Tre donne intorno al cor mi son venute* (Three ladies have gathered round my heart), an important work from the period of exile, probably the fifteenth treatise was to deal with the *sirventes* against avarice, *Doglia mi reca ne lo cor ardire* (Grief brings boldness to my heart); the subjects of the other sections are uncertain. In regard to the whole, we may safely assume that it was to contain a doctrine of the good earthly life, as led by men who are noble in the new classless sense; perhaps the completed treatises are no more than an introduction, for a general plan cannot be derived from them, and it is scarcely conceivable that Dante had no systematic plan.

Dante attached great importance to the work, as we may judge from its length alone, for the completed sections amount to no more than a quarter of the projected whole. Why then did he abandon it? One need only consider the *Comedy* to gain an idea, but the answer is hard to formulate. There can be no doubt that the project of the *Comedy* replaced it in his mind, but the chronology of that development is not so simple, for the idea of the great poem, at least as a vague plan, must have been with him at an early date, before the exile, while on the other hand, he did not presumably do much of the actual writing until a good deal later, in the last years of his life. It seems likely that in the early years of exile Dante had both plans in mind, but postponed realization of the poem, the more ambitious and difficult task, out of awe at the immensity of the undertaking; but that, as the *Convivio* progressed, it left his creative drive more and more dissatisfied, so that work on the *Comedy* became an urgent necessity for him and he set the prose treatise aside. We shall try to explain here why the *Convivio* could not satisfy him.

First of all, the outward form was incompatible with his need for unity. Even if we assume that he had a systematic over-all plan, fifteen treatises, each one a commentary on a different poem, could not follow out a superordinate principle in keeping with the unified world view that he wished to set forth. That failing is certain to have irritated Dante's inborn sense of concordance and correspondence, which had been intensified by his philosophical studies; moreover, it ran counter to his striving for poetic power, for from the first it had been his way to build up an overpowering effect by progressive formal concentration. For the same reasons the individual treatises could not satisfy him; the discursive commentary form compelled him to follow the movement of the canzone far too mechanically, to observe an order which was justified in the poem but which, dislocated by frequent edifying digressions, often prevented him from building up solidly to a planned effect.

Again, the form of the *Convivio* implied too narrow a view of his subject. Here our attention is drawn to three considerations; personal, political, and philosophical. Of course they are inseparably linked, and we distinguish them only in order to clarify the picture as a whole. In the *Convivio* Dante takes the attitude of a teacher; in the treatises his personal experience, which is the subject of the canzoni, of the two first at least, ceases to be the essential and becomes a mere handle on which to hang his object lesson. Such "objectivization" is not at all in keeping with his inner purpose; for to Dante whatever knowledge he can attain and impart is passionate personal experience; the divorce of his personal destinies from his teaching, made necessary by the ex-

79

cessive rationality of the commentary form, was bound to become more and more burdensome, for as he grew older, in forced
isolation from the great events of the day, he began once more to
reflect on himself and resumed his old poetic habit, now enriched
by knowledge and experience, of weaving his own individual life
into the general fabric of events. Thus the objective, didactic attitude of the *Convivio* no longer satisfied his inner needs. The
uncontested triumph of philosophy over the love-mysticism of his
youth, which is dealt with in the second treatise and provides
the foundation of the whole work, had gradually ceased to reflect
his true inner situation, the true relation of spiritual forces within
him. It is impossible to describe the hidden process of transformation and rebirth that had meanwhile exalted the image of
Beatrice to a far higher rank, but we know from the *Comedy*
that such a transformation occurred. One cannot doubt that it
became more and more difficult for him to work on a project
begun in so very different a frame of mind.

Several times in the course of his exile Dante was to conceive
political hopes, particularly on the occasion of Henry VII's Italian campaign; but they were always deceived and to the end he
preserved the attitude in which he has survived in the memory
of men. In its poignant mixture of lonely pride and lonely help-
lessness, of willfulness and constraint, of yearning and inflexi-
bility, that attitude of his seems fated and necessary in an exem-
plary, monumental sense. Beyond a doubt he was the wisest,
most resolute man of his time; according to the Platonic principle which is still valid wherever a man is manifestly endowed
with the gift of leadership, he was born to rule; however, he did
not rule, but led a life of solitary poverty. To correct and overcome that disharmony of fate, not by Stoic asceticism and renun-
ciation, but by taking account of historical events, by mastering
them and ordering them in his mind—that was the task to which
his character drove him. Here again it was inevitable that the
conceptual, unconcrete, purely contemplative, and didactic attitude of the *Convivio* would soon strike him as inappropriate and
in a way false; the longer and the more keenly he suffered his
hard fate, the deeper became his self-awareness, his perception of
his extraordinary genius, impelling him to judge and to guide
concrete earthly reality through artistic creation.

Finally, he was bound to realize, in the course of his work on the *Convivio,* that there was a more complete, more unified, and more penetrating way of achieving his philosophical aim: a concordance between the mysticism of the *stil nuovo* and the Thomist-Aristotelian view of the world. Starting from a line in a canzone, he was obliged in the *Convivio* to embark on a long and complicated digression when he wished for example to bring up the doctrine of the angels or of the virtues or of beatitude; then a harsh and barren transition would be needed to take him back to his starting point. The memory of the ancient poets, whom he often cites, must have made the awkwardness of such techniques extremely distasteful to him. They too in his belief had been teachers of wisdom, concealing an allegorical didactic message behind the concrete literal meaning of their verses; how far he went in that vulgar-spiritualist interpretation is shown by examples in the *Convivio* which strike us as almost grotesque; as for example when he interprets Aeneas' parting from Dido as an allegory for *temperantia.*[11] Because the ancient poets had embodied doctrine in events, had given it real, concrete form, their works were far more universal in appeal than any philosophical treatise; he had to follow their example, because like them he was a poet. And inevitably he regarded the Thomist-Aristotelian philosophy—which starts from sensory perception, which insists so strongly on the particularity of perceptible earthly forms and builds up an imaged, hierarchical universe—as the best possible material for a poetic work.

However, Dante's reflection on the ancient models, even if we try to read and interpret them as he did, does not suffice to explain the form of the *Comedy.* It is essentially a product of Dante's life and time; he chose that form because it was wholly in keeping with his inner purpose. The vision of the hereafter, the journey to the other world, was a common tradition of the Middle Ages. Since 1874 when Alessandro d'Ancona published his book on the precursors of Dante's *Divine Comedy,* scholarship has unearthed a vast amount of material that may have influenced or inspired Dante in writing the *Comedy;* quite recently an Arabist, Asín Palacios, in his work on Moslem eschatology in the *Divine Comedy,*[12] has broadened our approach to the question and exploded a number of generally accepted ideas; in his large handbook Vossler has critically examined the entire material and provided a survey of the present state of research on the subject. It cannot be proved that Dante was acquainted with any definite medieval sources and made use of them. But obviously the general idea and many of the mythical details stem from the rich treasure of mythology of Eastern as well as Western origin, that had accumulated over the centuries in the countries of the Mediterranean basin. That treasure was accessible to Dante without literary models; it was part of the air he breathed. It is true that writers of the very next generation were baffled by such material; their interpretations of it are often uncertain and contradictory. That, however, cannot be taken as an argument against our thesis, for their uncertainty, like ours, relates not to the mythical material, but to its significance within the poem. The question of literary models has nothing whatever to do with the inner genesis of the *Comedy*. In the second canto of the *Inferno* Dante mentions only Aeneas and St. Paul as having been empowered by divine grace to take that journey before him. That means, as the context also indicates, that he regards as legitimate precursors only great men whose vision occurred at a crucial turning point in history; if he was acquainted with any of the medieval visions of the other world, he assuredly did not have them in mind and did not look upon them as models when he undertook to write the *Comedy*. If any trace of them entered into his work, he arrived at it not through literature but in the indirect way to which we have just referred.

The convention of the journey to the other world offered Dante's passion for concrete expression and metaphysical order the possibilities which he himself had been unable to realize in his previous work and which those of his precursors who had composed eschatological visions had not even attempted to exploit. His life had been bitterly unhappy and full of dangerous crises; his convictions regarding the "right order" had come into conflict with the powers of the day; they had suffered defeat, but within him they remained in every sense unbroken; his own experience strengthened him and formed him, and his constant reflection on it gave rise to an almost uncanny and quite unprecedented insight into the historical process and the material of earthly history, that is, the characters and fates of the participants in their extreme individuality. As we have seen, his early poetry shows a keen eye for living reality; but it was the political catastrophe and its consequences, through which his own destiny became meaningful, which gave that aspect of his personality and talent their full intensity—for him political disaster was the *subito movimento di cose,* the sudden outward change[13] which invariably produces a grave inner crisis. He overcame the crisis and it vastly enriched his personal experience. He had lived in the very midst of important events, participating in them and suffering through them; in moments of extreme tension he had watched others acting, and often no doubt he had looked on with the feverish expectancy that sharpens all the senses; as an impoverished exile he was still in the direct presence of events, and now his experience was not attenuated by the comforting routine, the familiar surroundings of life in his home city, by the unquestioned esteem in which he was held there, in short all the factors which, in a secure life, make outward events seem more remote. So that now, when he inwardly evoked the lives and acts he had witnessed or learned of by hearsay, his acute eye, his keen intelligence, his profound piety and sense of hierarchical order, his spontaneous hatred of injustice, combined with his new experience.

Another consideration that is decidedly important for the genesis of the *Comedy* is that his material was eminently ready for use. In the century preceding the great poem, in which most of the events it treats took place, human lives had everywhere, but particularly in Italy, become freer and more varied than before, men's gestures had cast off their old rigidity. The phenomenon has often been described; this is not the place to go into its sociological and psychological causes, but one can easily convince oneself of its existence by comparing the legend of St. Francis with earlier legends of saints, the tales of the Novellino with their historical prototypes, Salimbene's chronicle, perhaps, with earlier Italian chronicles, by considering the colorful dramatic quality of Florentine history,[14] and finally, by noting the sudden emergence of living expression in the arts and looking into its causes. Whole groups of people who had hitherto lived in silent obscurity, began to achieve self-awareness, to emerge into the light of day and display their individual gestures; the long buried ancient tradition regarding the portrayal of outward and inner happening had reawakened.

But what was most decisive for so strictly rational and systematic a thinker as Dante, writing when he did, was that the philosophical doctrine he followed[15] set great store by individual forms and seemed to justify their portrayal. St. Thomas explained the diversity of things through the theological tenet that the world was made in God's image. In view of the fundamental imperfection of created things and of their essential dissimilarity to God, no *one* species of created things can possibly achieve likeness to God. Accordingly a diversity of created things becomes necessary, in order that in their totality they may approach a perfect likeness to God. Here I should like to quote from one of the passages stating that view, a few sentences in which it is summed up:

> Hence we must say that the distinction and multitude of things come from the intention of the first agent, who is God. For He brought things into being in order that His goodness might be communicated to creatures, and be represented by them; and because His goodness could not be adequately represented by one creature alone, He produced many and diverse creatures, that what was wanting to one in the representation of the divine goodness might be supplied by another. For goodness, which in God is simple and uniform, in creatures is manifold and divided; and hence the whole universe together participates the divine goodness more perfectly, and represents it better than any single creature whatever.[16]

Thus, in regard to Creation as a whole, diversity is looked upon not as an antithesis to perfection, but rather as an expression of it; the universe, moreover, is regarded, not as static but as engaged in a movement which is the movement of its forms toward self-realization, and in the perpetual striving from potency to act, diversity is exalted as the necessary road to perfection. As applied specifically to man in the Thomist psychology, that doctrine becomes a justification of the historical process with its concrete realities and dramatic tensions. For man, as a substantial union of soul and body, the soul being the form of the body, is not merely subject to the general formal distinction and material individuation of all created things, which possess diversity of essence but not freedom of action; in addition to Being, body, life, and senses, he also possesses intellect and will. Although the soul is bound to the body and needs it in order to function, it nevertheless possesses, situated as it is between the corporeal and the "separate" forms, special capacities, namely the ability to know and to will. Accordingly, man differs from the lower forms of creature, whose efficacy is wholly determined by the act of Creation, and also from the separate substances, the angels, who in a single first act of their own have turned toward God or away from Him. Man alone of the substantial entities possesses freedom, which operates in the time and space of his earthly existence; freedom is his principle of individuation, the moving principle of the *actus humanus*. His will necessarily strives toward the good as such; however, he never confronts that one good but individual goods;[17] and here lies the cause of the diversity of his action. Man's reason is manifested in reflection and judgment, his will in consent and choice (*electio*). The practical mechanism of the doctrine, as it affects the individual man, is supplied, according to Thomas, by the *habitus*. That is an acquired attribute, not the substance of man himself, but an enduring disposition which enriches and modifies the substance; it is the residuum in man's soul of his soul's history; for every action, every exertion of the will toward its goal leaves behind a trace, and the modification of the soul through its actions is the *habitus*. In the Thomist psychology diversities of *habitus* account for the diversity of human characters; it is the *habitus* which determines how each empirical man will realize his essence. It illumines the relations between the soul and its acts; it presupposes time and defines the inner development of man in time, thus making it clear that man requires a temporal process, history or destiny, in order to fulfil himself.

Not only is Dante's use of the Thomist-Aristotelian psychology evident in many theoretical passages in the *Convivio* and the

Comedy;[18] but, what is more, it provides the philosophical background and foundation of his poetic endeavor to portray the individual character or soul as forcefully as possible through the gestures of the body attaching to it. Some readers may be reluctant to accept a rational explanation of a poetic gift. But in poetic creation all the powers of the soul are effective, and when it is considered that after centuries in which expressive gesture was either wholly neglected or permitted only as comic by-play in popular literature, a poet imbued with the Thomist conception of the unity of body and soul was able to breathe the highest ethos and pathos into physical expression, the connection is difficult to deny. Dante was the first thinker-poet since antiquity to believe in the unity of the personality, in the concordance of body and soul; and so it was that reason reinforced his power to portray a man in the attitude and gesture which most fully sum up and most clearly manifest the totality of his *habitus*.

However, the men who appear in the *Comedy* are already removed from earthly time and temporal destiny. Dante chose for his representation a very special setting which, as we have said above, opened up wholly new possibilities of expression to him and to him alone. Sustained by the highest authorities of reason and faith, his poetic genius ventured to undertake what no one had undertaken before him: to represent the entire earthly, historical world of his knowledge and experience as already subjected to God's final judgment, so that each soul occupies the place assigned to it by the divine order. However, the individual figures, arrived at their ultimate, eschatological destination, are not divested of their earthly character. Their earthly historical character is not even attenuated, but rather held fast in all its intensity and so identified with their ultimate fate.

Before we look into the ramifications and consequences of that idea, which is the cardinal point of our investigation, we must defend it against a possible objection. According to universal Christian doctrine, the soul does not meet its ultimate fate immediately after death; the final destiny of all men is ushered in at the end of time, with the Last Judgment; during the period intervening between death and the Last Judgment, the soul is separate from the body, hence bereft of senses and bodily expression. However, St. Thomas, with most of the Church Fathers, held that the souls (with the exception of those requiring purification in Purgatory) arrived immediately after death at their final destination, assigned them according to their deserts. At the Last Judgment the happiness of the blessed and the sufferings of the damned are merely enhanced by the recovery of their bodies.[19] Dante follows that doctrine, which he formulates in the sixth canto of the *Inferno*.[20] A source of greater difficulty for St. Thomas was the disembodied state of the dead up to the Last Judgment, for it conflicted radically with his doctrine, derived from Aristotle, of a substantial union between body and soul. He was compelled to deny the soul at that stage the *perfectio naturae,* or natural perfection, it should have had as the natural form of the body; however, as a subsistent principle (for it is not a part, but the form of the body) it retained its being after separation from the destroyed body; and the *esse compositi,* or being of its composite, remained unchanged, for the being of the form is identical with the being of the matter, namely the *esse compositi,* or being of the composite.[21] Quite similarly in Dante, the soul separated in death from the body preserves its vital and sensitive faculties "virtually."[22] Dante also follows St. Thomas in determining the place allotted to the various souls.[23] It is only a short though significant step further to make the vital and sensitive faculties shape the surrounding air into a shadow body. With that license, perhaps Dante's most serious deviation from dogma,[24] he found his way back to the mythical tradition of an underworld peopled by shades and was enabled to use it for his poetic designs.

Thus what Dante sets forth in the *Comedy* is indeed the ultimate fate of his characters; their earthly term has run out and aside from those in Purgatory they are already at their allotted place, which they will occupy forever. As for the souls in Purgatory, their ultimate fate is also irrevocably decreed, though temporarily suspended; but since their purification is a consequence of their earthly conduct, it forms a part of their ultimate destiny, a necessary component of the final judgment; consequently, all the figures in the poem reveal the state which divine judgment, drawing up the balance-sheet of their lives, has assigned to them.

And in giving them shadow bodies, Dante has not only given them the possibilities of pleasure and pain; above all he has enabled them to stand in sensuous concreteness before him and before us, and to manifest their state by their physical presence. Thus there is something quite miraculous in what the reader of the poem feels to be self-evident (and in the last analysis, it actually is self-evident), namely, that the situation and attitude of the souls in the other world is in every way individual and in keeping with their former acts and sufferings on earth; that their situation in the hereafter is merely a continuation, intensification, and definitive fixation of their situation on earth, and that what is most particular and personal in their character and fate is fully preserved. The other eschatological visions that have come down to us, whether from ancient or Christian times, represent entirely different conceptions. Either they immerse all the dead in the levelling semi-existence of the realm of shades, in which the individual personality is destroyed or enfeebled, or else they separate the good and the saved from the wicked and damned with a crude moralism which resolutely sets at naught all earthly relations of rank. The idea of preserving a unity of character and dignity at every level of the otherworldly hierarchy, even the lowest, was utterly remote from them. Even the internal division of the precincts of the other world according to groups of sins and virtues, which seems to have been rather highly developed before Dante, particularly in Mohammedan eschatology, is only a classification by types, not by individuals, and there is no attempt whatever to preserve the earthly, individual form. At most we may say that these systems of the other world, many of which are based on Aristotelian ethics, contain potentially, and thus seem to call for, what is actually embodied in Dante's *Comedy*. Dante had no true precursors, except for the sixth book of the *Aeneid,* from which he derived not only his lofty didactic style, but also his way of finding ordered principle in events, though in these respects the student left the master far behind him. To anticipate the chief difference between them, Virgil, who lacked a unified doctrine and was unable to achieve a complete fusion between the philosophical and the mythical traditions, did not disclose ultimate destinies in his underworld; for the overwhelming majority of his souls were destined to embark on a new earthly existence, to enter into new bodies. That creates an entirely different background: by permitting one and the same soul to live several lives on earth in different bodies, transmigration destroys both the Christian drama of a unique term of earthly life, in which the decision must be made, and the ineluctable unity of the personality, the common form and fate of soul and body, attested in the doctrine of resurrection. But although the existence of Virgil's underworld figures is not intensified and definitive but diminished and transitory, although they are vagrant intangible shadows—a judgment borne out by the totally un-Dantesque *nulli certa domus*[25] (none of us has a fixed abode)—even so the direction of Dante's vision is implicit in that of Virgil. Perhaps in view of the imperfect composition of the book, in which critics have long distinguished a number of heterogeneous components, we should not be justified in taking at their face value the words of Anchises, *quisque suos patimur manes*[26] (each of us suffers the fate ordained by his own daemon), were it not for the meeting with Dido whose life in the underworld is a continuation of her earthly destiny. True, it is the living Aeneas who summons up the past, while Dido turns away in silence; but her attitude and the words of Aeneas that are the immediate cause of her silent flight—"I could not know that my departure would give you such grief as this"[27] —make it poignantly clear that this is a continuation of her personal destiny. Even here, to be sure, Virgil does not create what we should regard as a concrete, consistent character; he does not even attempt to do so. With the mention of Sichaeus, Dido's former husband, to whom she returns, the whole scene takes on a shadowy unreality. However, the meeting of the living Aeneas with the dead queen whom he had abandoned, the finest example of sentimental poetry known to Dante, must have made a profound impression on him. What for Virgil's noble Mantuan soul may have been little more than an isolated vision of passion became linked in Dante's mind with the ideas and happenings that formed the basis of his own view of the world; Virgil, the poet who had glorified the Roman Empire and prophesied the coming of Christ became his guide; the sixth book was for him authentic poetic truth, Aeneas his true precursor on the mysterious path through the underworld; and the Virgilian atmosphere flowed into his work, where to be sure it was profoundly affected by the power of Dante's own genius. Thus it would not be quite correct to say that Dante was influenced by Virgil; rather, he incorporated in his work a Virgilian element that he had thoroughly transformed.

What radically distinguishes the *Comedy* from all other visions of the other world is that in it the unity of man's earthly personality is preserved and fixed; the scene of action thus becomes the source of its poetic value, of its infinite truth, of the quality of direct empirical evidence which makes us feel that everything that happens in the work is real and credible and relevant to ourselves. The earthly world is encompassed in the other world of the *Comedy;* true, its historical order and form are destroyed, but in favor of a more complete and final form in which the destroyed form is included. For, as St. Thomas says: "When a more perfect form supervenes, the previous form is corrupted: yet so that the supervening form contains the perfection of the previous form, and something in addition."[28] It was necessary to destroy the form of the earthly world, for its potentiality, its striving for self-realization, and consequently its variability attain full term and cease in the after-life; the new form possesses everything that the former one possessed, and something more in addition, namely full actuality, immutable Being. Thus Dante undertook to portray the human beings who appear in the *Comedy* in the time and place of their perfect actuality, or in modern terms in the time and place of their ultimate self-realization, where their essence is fulfilled and made manifest for ever.

In our Introduction,[29] we said that Greek tragedy, unlike the Homeric epic, discloses the extremity at which there is no longer any diversity or potentiality, at which man's fate, already interpreted, is revealed to him, confronting him as something destructive, hostile, and seemingly alien; that the content of the tragedy is the hero's final struggle with his daemon, which so divides and consumes him that nothing remains of his personality but his age, race, class, and the most general traits of his temperament. With a certain artifice—by "artifice" I mean no untruth but a radical antithesis employed to bring out the most universal truth—the tragic poets, Sophocles in particular, displayed a struggling hero resisting his fate by action and reason; they shattered the unity of his personality, set the man apart from his fate, but only in order to reunite them the more compellingly at the moment of doom. That accounts for the greatness and also for the limits of their mimesis, their power of realistic portrayal. The ultimate fate in tragedy is death or something approaching it, and that most universal fate, once it so much as appears in the distance, removes the hero from the solid earthly ground on which he thinks he is standing, reduces his former existence and activity to nothingness, and concentrates his entire being in the special situation of the end. What happens at the end is, as it were, the mechanism of a power acting from without, which executes the decree of fate. Thus the tragedy presents the individual ethos in its ultimate and extreme concentration, but the hero is in an extraordinary situation different from his total earthly reality, and he relinquishes the situation only in dying. What happens afterward remains in the dark; in any case it is not self-realization, but rather an escape of the hero from himself into the realm of shades.

These remarks on Greek tragedy give us a clearer and more complete idea of how Dante in the *Comedy* transcended tragic death by identifying man's ultimate fate with the earthly unity of his personality, and how the very plan of the work made it possible, and indeed confronted him with the obligation, to represent earthly reality exactly as he saw it. Thus it became necessary that the characters in Dante's other world, in their situation and attitude, should represent the sum of themselves; that they should disclose, in a single act, the character and the fate that had filled out their lives. The earthly entelechy of each person was fused with the idea of his self, and when it came to representing this earthly entelechy no image could be too crass, no utterance too immoderate; no limits were imposed on expression, for what would anywhere else have offended against artistic good taste was here justified as a manifestation of the divine justice meted out with perfect appropriateness to each individual. Dante's subject matter in itself gave him the utmost freedom and the profoundest obligation to make use of it; and all the historical knowledge of men, all the insight into other men's lives that his critical judgment, his sharp and passionate feeling had enabled him to amass, poured forth in the great poem. Its human content, the product of his singular genius and of his unhappy life, is enormous; he was able to enter into each of his characters without ceasing to be Dante; he was able to speak their thousand languages, and nevertheless it is always the language of Dante.

To us it is perfectly obvious that this mimesis with its range and depth was no longer subject to the Aristotelian laws and that it did not fit into any of the classical genres. In that it resembled all the Christian art of the Middle Ages, though more consciously and conspicuously because it was a great, systematic creation encompassing the whole universe. To Dante, however, that was not fully clear, and there is some uncertainty in his stylistic appraisal of his work. In line with the scholastic view, based on fragmentary recollections of antiquity, which prescribes a happy beginning and unhappy end for tragedy and the opposite for comedy,[30] he called it a comedy. He characterized its style as *remissus et humilis,* negligent and humble, because unlike the *Aeneid,* the *alta tragedia,*[31] or high tragedy, as Dante calls it, the *Comedy* is written in the vernacular in which even women converse.[32] On the other hand he states expressly and not without apologetic intent that Horace permitted authors of comedy to employ the language of tragedy on occasion,[33] and in many passages of the great poem he clearly shows that he was aware of creating a poem in the sublime style. In these passages he refers to it by a new term of his own coining as "the sacred poem," *il poema sacro* or *lo sacrato poema,* or simply as "the vision."[34] These critical utterances on his own work reveal a conflict between the traditional scholastic views and a perception, still vague and poorly formulated, of the true nature of his poem; from classical theory Dante took over only one principle, the *sibi constare,*[35] or consistency, of his persons; all other tenets had lost their literal meaning for him. If the Aristotelian definition is interpreted in the widest sense—and that is permissible, for so ancient a text, so charged with history, can only be taken as a formulation of a very old law, which is still valid but which it became necessary long ago to interpret very differently from what the legislator consciously intended—then we may say that Dante's vision is a tragedy according to Aristotle's definition. In any event it is far more a tragedy than an epic, for the descriptive, epic elements in the poem are not autonomous, but serve other purposes, and the time, for Dante as well as his characters, is not the epic time in which destiny gradually unfolds, but the final time in which it is fulfilled.

What is the relation between Dante's representation of reality and the visual arts of his time? It is difficult to give an even half-way satisfactory answer to the question and here we can touch on it only briefly.[36] Since Giovanni Pisano artists had developed a keener perception of the world, and it is possible to find certain parallels between Dante and the great master of the period, Giotto. For both of them happening had been reborn as a self-contained reality; in both we find an almost classical sense of rhythmical structure and a very similar blending of the underlying law with the sensuous particulars of the world, and it is also possible to discern or presume certain cultural influences common to them both. But that does not take us very far. The mimesis of the *Comedy* is so much deeper and wider in range, it reaches out so much further into the past and future than any individual work of art of the early *trecento* that no comparison is possible. A great number of works, not only of the *trecento* but of earlier and later periods, might, all taken together, be commensurable with the *Comedy*—the parallel with Giotto becomes impossible once Dante rather than Giotto is taken as the starting point. The *Comedy* is a free act, expressing the ideas and perceptions of many centuries in *one* voice; the painting of the time was still the work of artisans who carried out commissions within the limits of the traditional iconography. By that I do not mean to disparage Giotto—precisely because he was relatively unlearned, he was able to take a candid view of the concrete present and to create something equivalent to the *Volgare illustre*—but the boldness and independence of the plan underlying Dante's *Summa vitae humanae* was far beyond a painter of the *trecento*.

Thus the conception of the *Comedy* offered Dante the possibility of satisfying his profound desire to configure reality; and in no less degree it enabled him to fulfil his striving for systematic order. In that respect, too, the *Comedy* constitutes a terminal point and a parting of the ways. A whole century before Dante, scholastic philosophy with its striving for concordance had gone beyond the mechanical conceptions based on the traditions of late antiquity and on Vulgar Spiritualist allegory and, in the *Summa theologica* of Thomas Aquinas, had achieved an organic, systematic order.[37] It employs the method of listing and classifying, beginning with God and going on to deal with the creatures who have issued from Him. It is a didactic system, which, in accordance with its purposes, treats of its subject as in being and at rest. Dante transforms Being into experience; he makes the world *come into being* by exploring it; Wisdom sets creative powers in motion and becomes a poetic figure. Dante starts out with a man who has lost his way. Reason—not Aristotle, but Virgil—is sent to help him and leads him to the revealed truth, which enables him to see God. Thus, by reversing the order of the *Summa,* Dante discloses divine truth as human destiny, as the element of Being in the consciousness of erring man, who participates only inadequately in divine Being and is in need of completion and fulfillment. In that human mind Being takes on a character of tension as though it were a force in process of becoming. In the vast edifice of the world through which he journeys, Dante is the only personage to whom it has not yet been interpreted, either in its self-contained reality or in its relevance to himself. The pathos experienced at each station of the way concerns him personally, for each station is potentially a part of his own ultimate destiny.

These very general remarks are intended only to define and circumscribe the dynamic element in the poem; to recall that God is at rest, that His Creation moves along eternally determined, unalterable paths, while man alone must seek his decision in uncertainty; in the order of his poem Dante embodied the dramatic content of the doctrine, grounded in the Christian history of salvation and theoretically formulated by St. Thomas—a doctrine fundamental to European culture. Man alone, but

94

man in every case regardless of his earthly situation, is and must be a dramatic hero.

The journey to the other world also gave Dante the best possible frame in which to set forth the depth and breadth of human knowledge. In the eschatological sphere physics and ethics, or as we should say today, the natural and humane sciences, are no longer separate; here nature, too, is ordered by an ethical standard, the measure of its participation in divine Being, and every natural site has the ethical rank of the rational beings who dwell in it. With that the meaning of landscape is defined. The vivid descriptions of landscape in which the great poem abounds are never autonomous or purely lyrical; true, they appeal directly to the reader's emotions, they arouse delight or horror; but the feelings awakened by the landscape are not allowed to seep away like vague romantic dreams, but forcefully recapitulated, for the landscape is nothing other than the appropriate scene or metaphorical symbol of human destiny. However, a journey which reveals a world order in which nature and spirit are one, must also include all knowledge, insofar as that is a knowledge of Being and hence truth; for in a vision of this kind the poet comes face to face with true Being. Here, accordingly, Dante found a natural frame in which to encompass the whole range of his knowledge, and in every single instance his criterion of truth was: has it a place in the total system?

The same applies most particularly to the order of historical events which in the *Comedy* are represented as either already past and judged or else are predicted by the seers among the inhabitants of the three realms. The opinion has been put forward that Dante, under the influence of his personal misfortunes and of his violent temperament, was often unjust toward the persons he portrayed, especially if they had taken the opposing side in political events to which he attached importance. For several reasons, I believe that contention to be unjustified. By the time he began to write the *Comedy,* he had long ceased to belong to any political party and was bitterly opposed to everything that was happening in Italy. Moreover, there are many passages in which men who to his mind had pursued disastrous aims are appealingly portrayed, in all their human dignity. Above all it cannot be denied—and this is the essential point here—that every single judgment is based on a general philosophical and historical view, Dante's perspective of a God-given balanced order on earth. One may disagree with that view, and subsequent events did not confirm it. But there is no doubt that Dante held it and couched it in a systematic, ethical form which none of his contemporaries who calculated the course of events more correctly could equal and which, despite its failure in history, has even today, in an entirely different world, inspired some of the most lucid and authentic political and historical thinking. And the very fact that he held such a view is incompatible with the suspicion that personal rancor was a dominant factor in his judgment of persons. Finally, it should be considered that Dante is often our only source of information about the contemporaries he speaks of in his poem and in every case the only *effective* source; in other words, those men are remembered as Dante represented them. Thus there is no standard of comparison; we can only compare Dante's portraits of those figures with the pictures that have come down to us, that is, with themselves. In order to understand Dante's justice, that is, the hierarchical order of the persons in his other world, we must bear in mind that here, at the scene of their ultimate destiny, they appear singly and not in their mutual relations; they are employed only as material, from which Dante selects what he needs for his definite purpose; each man is judged singly, according to his direct relation to the world order, his significance in the world order is alone decisive.[38] Here again we see how well the idea of a journey to the hereafter fits in with Dante's order of the world. In the hereafter historical ties are dissolved, the character and unity of the individual are preserved, but historical place and earthly rank are lost; in that transformation, in which the immanent world is as it were taken apart and put together anew, the crucial question in regard to each individual is: what bearing did his historical activity as a whole have upon the ultimate goal of Creation? That becomes particularly evident when we consider historical figures who were closely connected with each other, such as Caesar's enemies, who include Cato; Dante utterly disregards the relations of those men to one another, interprets each man individually and assigns to him the place befitting him in view of the goal of the world.

Also on the aesthetic level, in respect to composition, versification, and language, his subject demanded the order which he himself wished to give, and had the ability to give, to his life work. As it unfolds before the traveller, the after-life reveals to him the final structure in which all the parts of the world are ordered in respect to God; his account of his experience must reflect, faithfully and completely, the system of relations and concordances contained in the divine plan. Thus the composition of the poem, of which I shall speak in detail in the next chapter, is imposed by the subject matter. The other aesthetic problem was to find a style appropriate to the subject matter. All his life Dante had been working toward a solution, and the noble style in which the poem is written is a harmony of all the voices that had ever struck his ear. All those voices can be heard in the lines of the *Comedy,* the Provençal poets and the *stil nuovo,* the language of Virgil and of Christian hymns, the French epic and the Umbrian Lauds, the terminology of the philosophical schools and the incomparable wealth of the popular vernacular which here for the first time found its way into a poem in the lofty style. But the power to combine such diverse elements, to make them merge, with no effect of oddity or disparity, into a continuous flow, a language full of supple strength and natural dignity: that power too Dante received from his superhuman subject which did not, like a man or a human event, have to be exalted or amplified in order to become sublime; for in itself it is sublime and all-encompassing: highest and lowest, wisdom and folly, abstract concept and concrete thing, feeling and event— all have their legitimate place in it. They are all contained in Creation and must be represented with their natural expression; here there is nothing to exalt and nothing to conceal, for the truth of things is their dignity once they are contemplated and described in their relation to the order of the Creator. Dante's subject matter freed him from linguistic restrictions by automatically justifying and exactly defining the linguistic expression conforming to each thing; for any excess, any disproportionate or purely sensuous indulgence in virtuosity would have run counter to his purpose and shattered his order. However skillful, it would have been quite unacceptable—far more so than in the treatment of an earthly theme. In the language of the *Comedy* order and reality reflect and enrich one another in a way that seems all the more amazing in view of the strict and intricate versification within which Dante moves with virtually no apparent effort. Except where an unusual meaning calls for a special kind of expression, the sentences are simple, clear and firm, seldom departing from a natural structure for the sake of rhyme or metre; they lie embedded in the intricate *terza rima* as though it were the natural rhythm of human speech. To Dante it was self-evident that the *Comedy* must be written in Italian, and in view of the passage we have quoted from the *Convivio*[39] his decision required no further justification, although even in Dante's lifetime the representatives of a dawning humanism expressed surprise at his choice.[40] To Dante culture and tradition were inseparable from the living present; cultivation took in all branches of knowledge, but it was not the apanage of the learned, and his conception of the noble, derived from the *stil nuovo,* was a movement of the heart carrying no implication of learned contempt for the *profanum vulgus,* the common crowd; the highest knowledge must be set before every man, and only by drawing on the everyday language and the everyday lives of men could he fashion a sublime style capable of universal expression. Thus he founded the national literature of his country and with it the lofty European style underlying the literature of all the national tongues; if the humanists had taken up his heritage, the eternal and still unresolved *querelle des anciens et des modernes* would probably never have arisen.

We conclude with the most important point: the subject matter of the *Comedy* enabled and required Dante to justify his own unhappy life and to reconcile it with the universal order. The man gone astray of the opening lines is Dante; he himself is the traveller through the three realms, to whom the highest grace has sent a savior and guide. Beatrice descends into the underworld to summon Virgil, the guide, from his eternal abode. Two persons leave their place in the predetermined and fulfilled scheme in order to carry out the work of grace; and these two executants of the divine plan of salvation are at the same time the guiding forces in Dante's life: Virgil, poet of the *pax romana* and prophet of last things, bearer of a truth which to him was still veiled, gave Dante the fine style of an all-encompassing poetry of wisdom, while Beatrice, formerly a visible manifestation of the secret truth, now come forth as a revelation of the perfect order, was his own daemon, to follow and be saved or to turn away from and be damned. These are the deepest powers within him, the powers of his own true love, who have been summoned up to save him from error—and therein lies the justice of the grace that annuls the stern sentence.[41] They imbue him with courage to follow them, to tear himself away from the destructive powers, and they lead him toward intuitive knowledge of the divine order. Not only his past, but his future life as well, is interpreted and justified; for the time of the vision is the year 1300 when he was still living in Florence and the catastrophe was still to come; thus the error with which the poem starts precedes this date, and what follows—exile, vain hopes, poverty, proud withdrawal—has no connection with his error; they are his deserved and appropriate earthly fate, they belong to him like the dignity of a high office. You will suffer and be unhappy, say Brunetto and Cacciaguida; but remember only to be proud and to persevere in your stand; its rightness will be made manifest. With deep humility but full self-certainty Dante pits himself against his time in anticipation of earthly fame and beatitude in the hereafter.

The intervention of his transfigured loved one and his journey to her through Hell and Purgatory also signify the wanderer's return to the inspiration of his youth; the boy's first experience, his emotion at the sight of her, is repeated at the summit of Purgatory. His path leads from the senses through knowledge and destiny to a second, visionary experience of the senses; and in all its stations the divine order operates first as an overpowering intimation, then as an impulse of the will toward right action, and lastly as an apparition which fulfils his striving and reveals the intelligible. It is the road of every Christian man, who starts from the senses, who is endowed with reason as a dialectical principle which, in the drama of his earthly life, must make a decision between ever increasing participation and eternal defection. But the veiled mystery which is revealed at the end of the way, the secret sign which forever admonishes and commands him to follow, the daemon Beatrice, never ceases to be what she was in the beginning, namely a particular human being and a very personal, contingent experience; sensuous charm is made to further the work of salvation, and it is Love itself which raises man to the vision of God. In the ultimate after-life, outward appearance is not distinct from the idea but contained in it and transfigured. That is something which only poetry can aspire to express, and therein it surpasses didactic philosophy which cannot depart from reason. Poetry alone is close to revelation and capable of expressing it. Such poetry is more than beautiful illusion; it is no longer imitation, third in rank as to truth. Here revealed truth and its poetic form are one.

IV

THE STRUCTURE OF THE *COMEDY*

The structure of the great poem is made up of three merging, interwoven systems which are conceived of as corresponding in the divine order. There is a physical, an ethical, and a historico-political system; each of them, in turn, involves a synthesis of different traditions.

The physical system consists in the Ptolemaic order of the universe, as adapted to Christian dogma by Christian Aristotelianism; as a whole and in most of its details, that order was already formulated in the writings of the high scholastic philosophers and in the didactic works inspired by them, so that Dante was able to derive its basic traits from his sources—Aristotle, Alfraganus, Albertus Magnus, Thomas Aquinas, Brunetto Latini. The globe of the earth is at the center of the cosmos; round it revolve nine concentric celestial spheres, while a tenth, all-embracing sphere, the Empyrean, the seat of God, is conceived to be at perfect rest. Only half the earth, the northern hemisphere, is inhabited; the eastern and western limits of the οἰκουμένη, or inhabited world, are the Ganges and the Pillars of Hercules; its center is Jerusalem. In the interior of the earth, or rather of the northern hemisphere, like a funnel narrowing down toward the center of the earth, lies Hell; in its deepest part, at the very center of the earth, is the eternal abode of Lucifer, who in his fall immediately after the Creation, bored deep into the earth, pushing aside an enormous portion of its interior and driving it upward;[1] that portion of the earth is the great mountain which alone rises above the ocean which covers the whole southern hemisphere. It is the mountain of Purgatory, abode of souls headed for Paradise but still in need of purification. On the summit of the mountain, the point where the earth comes closest to the lowest celestial sphere,[2] lies the Earthly Paradise, where the first man and woman lived before the fall from grace. The celestial spheres, which are the true Paradise, are ordered according to the heavenly bodies situated in them; first the spheres of the seven planets of ancient astronomy in the order: Moon, Mercury, Venus, Sun, Mars, Jupiter, Saturn; then the sphere of the fixed stars; the ninth is the invisible crystalline heaven, and the last is the Empyrean. The motion of the celestial spheres is concentric and circular; a burning desire to be united with God imparts a circular motion of the highest velocity to the ninth sphere, that closest to the motionless Empyrean where He dwells; the ninth sphere in turn, through the hierarchy of Intelligences, or Angels, communicates its motion to the lower spheres within it.[3]

Within the heaven of the divine peace [the empyrean] a body whirls [the *Primum mobile,* or ninth heaven], in whose virtue lies the being of all that it contains [the entire cosmos]. The next heaven, which has so many things to show [the heaven of the fixed stars with its many luminaries], distributes this being among various essences, different from yet contained in it. The other spheres [the planetary heavens] by various differentiations bestow to their own ends the distinctions which they have within themselves, together with the seeds. These organs of the world move, as you now see, from step to step, receiving from above and acting on what is below. . . . The movement and virtue of the holy spheres must be inspired by the blessed movers [the intelligences, or angels], like the hammer's art by the smith; and heaven, which so many lights make fair [the heaven of the fixed stars], takes the stamp from the profound mind that turns it and makes of that stamp a seal. And as the soul within your dust is diffused through differing members shaped to different functions, so the Intelligence [i.e., God] unfolds its goodness multiplied through the stars, itself revolving upon its unity. Different virtues make different alloys with the precious bodies that they quicken [the starry heaven], to which they are bound like life in you. Because of the happy nature from which it derives, the virtue shines, mingled, through the body like joy through a living eye. From this comes what seems different between one light and another, not from density or rarity. This is the formal principle. . . .[4]

From this passage we learn the following points:

1. The Being and the entire motion of the universe stem from the *primum mobile* or prime mover (hence from God's love as well as from the love of God). All Creation is an unfolding and reflection of divine Being—*non è se non splendor di quella idea che partorisce amando il nostro sire*[5] (it is nothing but the reglow of that Idea which our Sire, in loving, begets); its motion and all its activity have their eternal source in Him. The lines translated above are drawn from a passage about the nature of the Moon and that is why they speak only of the celestial spheres. Actually the same is true of all Creation, both of that part which is created directly by God (intelligences, celestial spheres, *prima materia,* and the human soul) and of that part which is produced indirectly through His organs (elements, plants, animals).[6] Everywhere it is *la divina bontà che 'l mondo imprenta*[7] (the divine goodness which stamps the world), and the motion it produces is Love: *Nè creator nè creatura mai . . . fu sanza amore, o natural o d'animo* (Neither creator nor creature . . . was ever without love, either natural or rational).[8]

2. The universe is a multiplication of the first motion; the Intelligences, or Angels, communicate it to the lower degrees of Creation and impart to all created things the energy and motion peculiar to them, but in spite of all that the unity of divine Being is never relinquished: the Trinity, as Dante quotes St. Thomas as saying:[9]

> *per sua bontate il suo raggiare aduna*
> *quasi specchiato, in nove sussistenze,*
> *etternalmente rimanendosi una.*

Quindi discende a l'ultime potenze
giù d'atto in atto, tanto divenendo,
che più non fa che brevi contingenze;
e queste contingenze esser intendo
le cose generate. . . .

(of its goodness focuses its own raying, as though reflected, in nine existences, eternally abiding one. Thence
it descends to the remotest potencies, down, from act to
act, becoming such as makes now mere brief contingencies; by which contingencies I understand the generated
things . . .).

Thus the source of the multiplicity of Creation is the unfolding
and reflection of divine goodness through the *nove sussistenze,*
or nine existences, that is, the Angels, who are the movers of the
heavenly spheres and of their luminaries. Here the relation between astrological conceptions and the divine order of the world
is made perfectly clear. In the first canto of the *Paradiso* Dante
expresses his surprise that he, as a material body, should have
been able to rise up to heaven, and Beatrice replies: *"Le cose
tutte quante hanno ordine tra loro* . . . : All things whatsoever
observe a mutual order; and this is the form that makes the
universe like God. In it the exalted creatures [those endowed with
intelligence] trace the impress of the Eternal Worth, which is
the goal for which the norm now spoken of was made. In the
order of which I speak all things incline, by various lots, nearer
or less near to their source; for which reason they move to different ports across the great sea of being, each one with instinct
given it to bear it on. This bears the fire toward the moon; this
is the mover in the hearts of things that die; this draws the
earth . . . together and unites it. This bow shoots not only the
creatures that lack intelligence but those that have both intellect
and love. The Providence that ordains all this, with its light
makes ever still the heaven in which that one whirls which has
the greatest speed; and there now, as to the site ordained, the
power of that bowstring bears us. . . ."[10]

This instinct is the work of the celestial spheres, *ovra de le
rote magne, che drizzan ciascun seme ad alcun fine*[11] (operation
of the mighty spheres that direct each seed to some end); the

whole of earthly Creation is subject to them with the exception of man; for although man as a body, and hence also the sensitive powers of the soul, are subject to inclination by the influence of the stars, he possesses in the rational part of his soul the power to guide and limit that influence; that power is his free will.[12] "The heavenly bodies," says St. Thomas,[13] "cannot be the direct cause of the free-will's operations. Nevertheless, they can be a disposive cause of an inclination to those operations, in so far as they make an impression on the human body, and consequently on the sensitive powers which are acts of bodily organs having an inclination for human acts." And similarly in another passage:[14] "The heavenly bodies are not the cause of our willing and choosing. For the will is in the intellectual part of the soul . . . the heavenly bodies cannot make a direct impression on our intellect. . . ." The *pars intellectiva* of the soul is man's *vis ultima*,[15] or ultimate essence, what makes him a man, and he must employ it for good or evil. Without it he could no more do evil than a plant or an animal: for *lo naturale (amore) è sempre sanza errore*. The natural is always without error.[16]

These remarks on the special position of man bring us to the second of the systems underlying the *Comedy,* the ethical system. Man alone possesses freedom of choice, a power compounded of intellect and will, which, though closely connected with the natural disposition and hence always individual, reaches out beyond it; it is that power which enables him during his lifetime on earth, to love in the right or wrong way and so decide his own fate. In the ethical system he builds up on the basis of that conception, Dante follows the *Nicomachean Ethics* as elaborated in St. Thomas. Brunetto Latini had set forth the ethical doctrines of Aristotle and St. Thomas in his *Trésor,* particularly in the sixth and seventh books. His exposition shows many points of contact with Dante, and the words *m'insegnavate come l'uom s'etterna*[17] (you taught me how man makes himself eternal) make it clear that Dante regarded Brunetto as the foremost authority on those ideas.

Man's ethical nature is grounded in his natural inclination or disposition. As such that is always good, for it is love, more specifically the love of some good. The highest good and the source of the good is God. The *anima rationalis,* or reason, can choose the immediate love of Him as the main goal of earthly life, and attain the highest earthly excellence through the virtues of the *vita contemplativa.* But reason, which is intimately bound up with the individual disposition, can also choose a mediated love of God and turn to His creatures, that is, to the particular earthly goods. That choice leads inevitably to an active life, which however may take very different forms; it is good as long as the intermediate, "secondary" goods are loved with due moderation, and then it leads to the virtues of the *vita activa.* Natural love, however, can be corrupted by immoderation or faulty choice of its object. Such corruption is sin, which always has its source in immoderate or misguided love.

In the Other World which Dante explores in his poem, men are already judged; the balance sheet of their lives is drawn and they are put in the place that is theirs forever; the physical character of each station accords with the ethical worth of its inhabitants. Some souls are damned; others, in Purgatory, savor the anticipation of a beatitude soon to come; still others possess it already. Within each of the three realms, the souls are arranged in groups corresponding to their earthly acts or dispositions. And within those groups each man who appears as an individual is represented in the attitude and dignity befitting his own particular life and character. Each of the three systems of classification—the three realms, their internal groupings, and within each group the individual character—has in itself an ethical significance, and sometimes the individual character becomes so intense as to outweigh the first two principles in determining Dante's—and our own—sympathies. That is of course particularly true in connection with the *Inferno;* even aside from the virtuous pagans, including Virgil, who dwell in Limbo, the *Inferno* is rich in significant figures whose extraordinary virtues are not annulled by the vice for which they have been damned; though perverted, the original drive toward the good is still so strong in them that they preserve all their humanity in our eyes and some of them stand foremost in our sympathies. Though Dante never says so explicitly, it seems to me unquestionable that the preservation of individual attitudes indicative of such dignity or the contrary should be looked upon as part of the eternal judgment.[18]

The principle of grouping is different in each of the three realms, as is only natural when we consider the different purpose pursued. In Hell, the realm of eternal punishment, there can be no classification by virtues, and in Paradise there are no sins or vices; in Purgatory there are both. There, since the purpose is purification, the basis of classification must be the evil impulses in need of expiation, but it cannot coincide with the classification of sins in Hell, for punishment is meted out for acts accomplished and not effectively repented, while purification applies to corrupt inclinations after individual acts have been confessed and repented. Sin, as we have seen, has its source in immoderate and misguided loves, which are classified according to the vicious dispositions they create in the soul. Immoderate love is broken down into a "too much" and a "too little." The too much involves the passion for earthly goods, hence lust, gluttony, and avarice; the too little is sloth. As to misguided love, it is directed toward evil. In the Thomist conception, however, evil is purely negative, since Creation as the diffusion of divine goodness can never in itself be evil; consequently misguided love can consist only in a desire to pervert the good, to turn away from its goodness, and since no one can hate himself, it is directed toward one's neighbor; it is a love of one's neighbor's evil and a "wishing of evil to one's neighbor"; its subdivisions are *superbia,* or pride,[19] *invidia,* or envy, and *ira,* or anger. That is the classification of the *Purgatorio,*[20] where the souls which have repented and confessed their sins are purified, and the stations ascend from the gravest to the most venial sins: the order is *superbia, invidia, ira, accidia, avarizia, gola, lussuria,* that is, pride, envy, anger, sloth, covetousness, gluttony, lust. When, on the other hand, we consider the sins punished in Hell, the evil deeds that have not been forgiven by God's grace, a new consideration enters in, the consent of the will, for without it no act can be carried out. Here, accordingly, the disposition of the will is the basis of judgment and classification. If after mature and careful reflection the will consents to an evil deed, we have a deed of pure wickedness (*malizia*); if reflection is clouded by an excess of desire, we have an act of passion (*incontinenza*). Thus Hell is divided into two sections according to the severity of the punishment; those who have sinned through passion are punished less severely than those who have sinned through wickedness, and here the descent is from the less to the more severe. That fundamental difference in the ethical order of the two realms—the fact that in the one evil deeds are punished, while in the other perverted dispositions are purified—explains why pride and envy have no groups in Hell, for they are dispositions with which no definite acts can be correlated. And it also explains why in Purgatory anger is represented as love of evil and assigned to the second, more grievous category, while in Hell it takes two forms: sudden anger, viewed as a sin of passion and assigned to the less severe section; and premeditated, vengeful anger, assigned to the lower circles of *malizia*. *Accidia,* or sloth, has no place in Hell proper, for it does not result in any action—it is the cowards of Limbo who correspond to the *accidiosi,* or slothful ones, of the fourth circle of Purgatory. In Paradise, finally, the souls are ordered according to their good, unperverted dispositions, their just and measured love: each class is situated in the sphere of the heavenly body whose influence for good their *anima rationalis* has preserved pure and in just measure, or which, if perverted, they have purified in Purgatory; each soul is assigned to the sphere of the heavenly body that has exerted the dominant influence upon him.[21]

The general classification of evil deeds in Hell is derived from the Aristotelian ethics; but in Limbo, in the first and sixth circles, and in many particulars elsewhere, other sources and conceptions are utilized. In devising punishments and inventing diabolical spirits, Dante's poetic fantasy works with a vast store of traditional mythology, whose sources and significance have repeatedly been investigated but never with wholly satisfactory results. The crater of Hell is divided into nine circles; the sins become more heinous and the punishments more terrible in descending order. The first circle harbors virtuous pagans and unbaptized children, both of which categories are barred from Paradise only because they are not Christians; it is not given them to see God, but that is their only punishment. The figures of antiquity move with a solemn dignity recalling ancient conceptions of the after-life. The second to fifth circles are occupied by those who have sinned from *incontinenza;* first those given to earthly passion—lust and gluttony—then those guilty of spiritual immoderation—avarice and anger. The fifth and last circle of the section is Styx, the river of Hell; Virgil and Dante cross it to enter the walled city of *malizia,* the true *civitas diaboli,* or city of the Devil. Here again the uppermost circle (the sixth) contains a category for which Aristotle did not provide, that of the heretics and godless "Epicureans"; then, in the Aristotelian order come the violent (seventh circle) and the deceivers (eighth circle), both groups being subdivided according to the special character of their sin and punishment. There are three classes of violence: against one's fellow man, against oneself, and against God. The deceivers, on the other hand, are subdivided according to concrete offenses: procurers, flatterers, simonists, fortune-tellers, swindlers (*barattieri*), hypocrites, thieves, evil counsellors, trouble-makers, forgers. Removed from the group and relegated to the ninth and lowest circle of Hell are those deceivers who have abused a sacred bond of trust: the traitors. In his three sets of jaws Lucifer, dwelling in the deepest abyss of Hell, grinds up the worst traitors: Judas who betrayed Christ, and Brutus and Cassius who murdered Caesar and betrayed the Imperium.

To Limbo Dante banished the vast multitudes of the cowardly and pusillanimous, *che visser sanza infamia e sanza lodo*[22] (who lived without blame and without praise), and with them those angels who did not take sides in the rebellion of Lucifer. The classification is perfectly natural because sloth begets no specific evil deeds and consequently does not fit in with the system of punishments in Hell, while, on the other hand, it is definitely regarded as a sin by Aristotle and St. Thomas, since without love a man cannot see God. But what strikes and appalls us in reading the *Comedy* is the intensity of Dante's contempt for those who were neither hot nor cold. Their punishment is not so much torment as loathsome molestation: running about noisily in circles they are stung by insects. But their moral suffering is far greater: Compassion and Justice turn scornfully aside from them; not a trace of them remains on earth, Heaven excludes them, and worst of all, they are not even in Hell *ch'alcuna gloria i rei avrebber d'elli* (for the wicked would have some glory over them). In a way they are inferior to the lowest category of sinners, who at least were men, doing good or evil in a human way, while these, the slothful and lukewarm "never lived," for they made no use of man's *ultima vis,* his capacity to act in accordance with the decision of his reason and will. With these words: *questi sciaurati che mai non fur vivi* (these unfortunate who never were alive), Dante accounts for their eternal fate; here as everywhere else the sinners are assigned their eternal abode in accordance with the law of appropriate retribution, of *contrapasso.*[23] But the violence of Dante's tone when he speaks of them reveals the very personal bias of a man who was passionate, fearless, and indomitable in his espousal of the good, and for whom active struggle was the natural form of life.

The law of appropriate retribution governs the system of punishments in Hell, giving rise to a very concrete and realistic allegorism which in turn provides suitable and varied backgrounds for the appearance of the various figures. The punishments are chosen with a fantastic and gruesome ingenuity which reveals the richness, the dark pathos, and the almost pedantically precise concreteness of Dante's genius. With all their evocative power and emotional overtones, there is never any vague impressionist suggestion in these landscapes of Hell. The exposition is always orderly and methodical, as in a realistic record, and even where he raises his voice to adjure, even where he arouses sympathy, anger, dread or horror in the reader, he never sacrifices the strictest clarity. The landscapes and punishments of Hell are the basis of the fame that Dante has enjoyed in romantic periods and not entirely without justification they still have a good deal to do with the popular estimate of him. They were also the basis of the revulsion from him of strictly classicist periods. In the last analysis both points of view are misunderstandings. Dante was indeed one of the creators of Romanticism; his work was largely responsible for its fantastic Gothic dream world and for its exaltation of the horrible and grotesque; but he would not have been pleased with his followers. It was an Italian, Giambattista Vico, who, in a century hostile to Dante, gave expression for the first time to that form of admiration which culminated in the

Romantic aesthetics.[24] He compares Dante with Homer; both poets, he tells us, lived at a time when their peoples had just emerged from barbarism, and they mirrored the barbaric age in their poems; in bold, generous strokes they related true stories; both were endowed with a vigorous, naïve imagination, without a trace of the philosophical, rationalistic subtlety characteristic of civilized periods; Dante took the same naïve delight in the terrible punishments of Hell as did Homer in the cruel, bloody battles that are the sublime content of his *Iliad;* neither of them was in any sense a philosopher; their wisdom was the heroic, mythical wisdom of primitive, barbaric peoples. Here we shall not concern ourselves with the element of truth in that judgment from the early eighteenth century; what is astonishing is that Vico, who to be sure had no conception of the culture of the *trecento,* should not have been led to a more accurate view of Dante by comparison with Homer and by the actual text of Dante's work itself, which he had before him. He completely overlooked, or rather he was unwilling to accept, the fact[25] that the *Comedy* was a work of high Scholasticism, of *umana ragione tutta spiegata,* of human reason fully explained, and that Dante the barbarian was far superior in "intellectual subtlety," that is, in precision and clarity of thought to himself, Vico, who, though with distaste, had plowed his way through Scholastic, Jansenist, and Cartesian logic. Vico failed to see it because he was no more able to read what is clearly set forth in the text than were Dante's romantic admirers who have never wearied of citing the *Inferno* in support of their literary ideals, although even, or one might say most particularly, in the *Inferno* Dante's poetic power actually springs from a clear and precise intelligence, thoroughly disinclined to disorderly, sentimental effusion. In conceiving the punishments of Hell, Dante employs mythical material and elements of popular faith; they are enormously imaginative, but each single one of them is based on strict and precise reflection, on the rank and degree of the sin in question, on a thorough knowledge of rational systems of ethics; and each one, as a concrete realization of the idea of divine order, is calculated to provoke rational thought concerning the nature of this sin, that is, the way in which it deviates from the divine order. The slaves of desire are driven hither and thither by the storm wind; the gluttons cower on the ground in the cold rain; the sinners from anger battle one another in the swamp; the suicides are transformed into bushes torn bloody by a pack of hounds racing through them; the flatterers are stuck in human excrement and the traitors in eternal ice—such examples of Dante's rich imagery are not haphazard products of an irresponsible fantasy seeking to pile up horrors, but the work of a serious, inquiring mind which for each sin has chosen its appropriate punishment and which owes the compelling force and concreteness of its images to its conviction that its choice is just and in conformity with the divine order. The same applies to the mythical monsters which serve both as guardians and as heraldic symbols of the circles of Hell. Nowhere is Dante more "medieval" in the French romantic sense than in those creations; moreover, they are imbued with the spirit of the vulgar-spiritualist iconographers who, in their striving to make hidden historical and moral meanings concretely visible, blended and exaggerated mythological traditions in accordance with a principle that has been lost to us and represented demonic forces as monsters moving in a fantastic half world. Like the monsters and grotesque figures of Gothic sculpture which delighted Victor Hugo and his friends, those inventions of Dante show the survival of an antiquity strangely distorted by mixture with heterogeneous doctrines; but in Dante they have cast off the element of arbitrary fantasy that they may have in other works by artists who have either forgotten the rational meanings or been able to assimilate them only in a confused, incomplete way. For though at first sight Dante's creatures retain the undiminished horror of dark fantastic monsters, closer scrutiny reveals that the poet carefully apportioned and defined their meanings, so that they require no commentary but rather help to elucidate the text. Their meaning is almost always clear, and in one of the few passages of this kind that are not easily explained, Dante says expressly that a specific doctrine is concealed within the strange lines.[26]

As we have seen, the ethical order of the *Purgatorio* is governed by the Thomist-Aristotelian principle that the vices are perversions of love; in it particular offenses are no longer taken into account; the steps before the entrance gate and the words of the angel who opens it[27] symbolize the sacrament of confession, and it is only when the gate has been passed, when the soul, freed from earthly guilt and started on its final *conversio ad deum,* or conversion to God, is no longer accessible to temptation, that purification sets in and with it the healing of the soul's wounds. But before reaching the gate, Virgil and Dante pass through a region of waiting souls, who have not yet been admitted to Purgatory: those who died excommunicated and, whether from negligence or because they died suddenly and violently, repented only in death. Those waiting outside Purgatory also include the souls in the Valley of Princes, who ruled under the imperfect, still unfulfilled world order; at night the serpent of temptation comes to them; to ward it off they implore and obtain the divine aid of the two angels with swords. Here Dante is overcome by a miraculous sleep, during which the mysterious Lucia raises him up to the entrance gate: only now begins the actual path of purification through the seven circles surrounding the mountain. Here the souls are purged of their vices in the order explained above: *superbia, invidia, ira, accidia, avarizia, gola, lussuria.* In this conception the doctrine of *Amore* is fused with that of the seven deadly sins. Purification is effected in accordance with the Aristotelian principle of the golden mean (μεσότης); the souls strive against their sinful nature until they feel free from all failing; then they are able to continue their journey upward. Though in his choice of penances Dante naturally subjected himself to narrower limits than in devising the punishments of Hell, his images are no less concrete, and here again they are based on the sharpest rationality; and here again the landscape and surroundings are at every stage suited to the particular variety of purification. Surrounded by images, visions, voices, disclosing examples of virtue rewarded or vice punished, the souls are healed by suffering. The suffering that heals them is either, as in most cases, of a nature opposed to the ailment—the haughty are bowed beneath heavy burdens; the envious, transformed into blind beggars, support one another; the slothful race about at breathtaking speed; the gluttons waste away from hunger and thirst within view of food and drink; the lustful live in purifying fire—or else it is similar to the ailment, a concrete symbolization of the vice, and then the activity of the penitent is in painful contradiction to his good will—that is the case with the covetous, who are chained to the ground with their faces down, and with the wrathful who move in a cloud of dark smoke. Though the destinies exhibited in the *Purgatorio* are far less diverse than those of the *Inferno,* that does not in the least impair the continuity of the earthly personality. Each individual who speaks or even appears is not only a penitent belonging to this or that group, but also remains what he was on earth, Oderisi the illuminator, Buonconte the Ghibelline, Hugh Capet the prince, Statius or Arnaut the poet. For as with punishment in Hell, penance here is not something new and additional which submerges the character of the individual, causing him to disappear amid the throng of those charged with the same failing and the same penance, but an actualization of potentialities that were already contained in his earthly character and hence a continuation and intensification of that same character. Hence, despite the uniformity of the penance itself, individuality is preserved in the way the penance is borne and the way in which it is related to the events of the individual life. The individual life is not forgotten, but carried over into the penance, where it remains wholly present with all its particularity, its mental and physical *habitus,* its temperament and its actual striving.

On the summit of the mountain of Purgatory, in the *nobilissimo loco totius terrae* (the noblest place on the whole earth), lies the Earthly Paradise, where Adam and Eve were created and lived until the fall from Grace. Dante linked it with Purgatory on the basis of a tradition which, like the conception of Purgatory itself, originated in the Orient and was widely diffused in the Middle Ages; St. Thomas himself says that the Earthly Paradise was not an abode of the dead, but a place of passage.[28] As the scene of earthly bliss it could only be situated at the summit of completed purification, still a part of the earth but already freed from the natural conditions pertaining on earth and directly subject to the effects of the celestial motion.[29] But at the same time the region, to which Beatrice descends in order to receive Dante, represents the earthly perfection which he forsook when he turned away from her after her death; and consequently, it is only there, after all the degrees of purification have been absolved in Purgatory, that the particular penance and atonement, applying to Dante alone and relating to his fall from perfection, sets in. In his early youth Dante was distinguished by high divine grace, so that he seemed destined to the highest perfection that mortal man can attain; but after Beatrice's death and transfiguration, the light of her countenance was no longer able to keep him on the right way, and he turned away from her. Nowhere does Dante clearly reveal the exact nature of that apostasy; from the place of his confession and penance we can only gather this much, that the vices purged in the circles of Purgatory, though all or a part of them may have contributed to his falling-away, did not constitute the core of his error, which was, on the contrary, something entirely personal, peculiar to the extraordinarily favored poet; the text tells us that after the seeming loss of that highest good, he was seduced by other, lesser earthly goods, but the seduction cannot have been identical with any one of the vices of the *Purgatorio;* rather, it was an extraordinary sin such as can be committed only by one on whom extraordinary grace has been conferred. To serve as the place of atonement for that sin is one of the functions of the Earthly Paradise, which Dante lost by his falling away; another, no less appropriate function is to provide the scene for the great allegory of the world's history, the particulars of which we shall consider in connection with the historico-political system of the *Comedy;* only in the place of the first, uncorrupted earthly order and of man's fall from it could the second order and the second fall from it—and this was Dante's view of the world's history since the coming of Christ— be appropriately represented.

Re-created by his bath in Lethe and Eunoe, Dante, now under the guidance of Beatrice, embarks on the ascent to the heavenly spheres. They are the *paese sincero,*[30] the unsullied country, created directly by God, the abode of the redeemed souls. The ethical order of the *Paradiso* presents greater difficulties than those of the *Inferno* and *Purgatorio*. For one thing, the poet himself gives no systematic explanation of it corresponding to those contained in the eleventh canto of the *Inferno* and the seventeenth canto of the *Purgatorio;* another difficulty is that in the *Paradiso* the same souls make two appearances, ordered in two different and seemingly unrelated hierarchies, first in one of the revolving spheres and once again in the rose of the Emyprean. Consequently the *Paradiso* has provided exegetes with an almost unparalleled opportunity to exert their speculative ingenuity; to our mind their speculations have often been too ingenious and sterile for that very reason. Yet they have seldom been entirely unprofitable; even when it seems unsatisfactory as a whole, a penetrating explanation in the spirit of Scholastic theology is bound to deepen our understanding of the poem and its complex doctrinal implications and consequently to increase our sensuous and intellectual enjoyment of the *Comedy.* No lover of Dante can read Filomusi-Guelfi or Busnelli or Ronzoni, to mention only a few of the leading commentators, without benefit; nevertheless it seems to me that neither the theory of the seven gifts of the Holy Ghost, nor the theory of the degree of *Caritas,* important as the latter may be, can provide a truly exhaustive principle by which to explain the organization of the *Paradiso;* as soon as we attempt to apply any of them systematically, we run into difficulties that can only be mastered with the help of undue violence.[31] Nor does it seem likely that Dante would have employed a single theory for the whole *Paradiso* without explicitly expounding it in a central passage. Though it is permissible to regard the entire *Summa theologica* as a source of information about Dante's thinking, it is dangerous to draw on specific dogmas from it in solving particlular problems unless Dante himself refers to them, for he never conceals the dogmatic foundations of his work.

The spheres of Heaven through which Dante is raised to the presence of God, are not, like the circles of Hell or the degrees of Purgatory, the actual abode of the souls Dante meets there; they make their appearance in one of the spheres only in order to give Dante a clear idea of their rank in the heavenly hierarchy; their actual dwelling place, their ultimate destiny, is beyond all places, in the congregation of the blessed, that is, in the white rose of the Empyrean.[32] Here again the hierarchy of the blessed is described, but what is said of it—the throne of the Emperor Henry, the division into saints of the Old and of the New Covenant, the partition between them, the blessed children, the two summits Mary and John the Baptist, and those who sit closest to them— does not refer directly to the ethical order of the world, but represents the goal of the history of salvation and thus pertains to the historico-political order. Of course the two orders cannot be looked upon as distinct, they must coincide, and it is evident that the great patricians of the realm, the roots of the rose, occupy the highest place from the standpoint both of historical providence and of ethical dignity; at the summit the identity of the two orders is actualized. But at least in the lower degrees, the ethical hierarchy of the white rose does not seem to be complete, unless we choose to round it out with the names of the Hebrew women and of the saints who occupy the ranks intermediate between the blessed of the old and of the new covenant. This has been attempted by various commentators, and some have tried to establish a thoroughgoing concordance between the hierarchy of the rose and that of the heavenly spheres; but the results are not satisfying. For though Dante sees "more than a thousand tiers"[33] in the white rose, he mentions only seven names on one side of the "partition" and three on the other, and says expressly—as one may gather from the whole presentation—that the series continues downward. The seven ranks represented by Mary-John, Eve-Francis, Beatrice-Rachel-Benedict, Sarah-Augustine, Rebecca, Judith and Ruth[34] necessarily constitute only the highest degrees of the hierarchy, and consequently cannot be brought into a parallel with the order of the heavenly spheres, which symbolizes the entire ethical order of Paradise. The attempts that have been made to overcome or to spirit away this difficulty strike me as too ingenious.

Consequently a complete ethical system of the *Paradiso* can be arrived at only on the basis of the celestial spheres where the blessed appear in order that their rank may be clear to Dante. Common to them all is beatitude through the vision of God, *visio Dei,* in which they all find peace; but from individual to individual the vision varies in degree, as it does with the "other host," the Angels, for it hinges on grace. None can know God fully, not even Mary or the highest ranks of the Angels; only God sees and knows Himself entirely. The degrees of the vision of God are based on grace, for the acquisition of which merit is a necessary but not a sufficient condition; grace is conferred freely and outweighs all merit, but to receive it is meritorious, for it can be received only with the help of good will. Grace engenders the vision; the vision determines the degree of celestial love, the *caritas patriae,* which in turn is manifested in the degree of light that the soul radiates. This order of rank is extremely subtle and ultimately each individual soul reflects it in its own way. By way of making the picture clear to himself and his readers, Dante has recourse to the astrological traditions of late antiquity. Since it is virtue that prepares the soul to receive grace, since virtue springs from earthly love of God, *caritas viae,* and since, moreover, the particular direction of this love is determined by natural predisposition, that is, by the influence of the stars, the right love, virtue, being the rational soul's right and moderate use of its natural predispositions, Dante found in the astrological classification of the natural predispositions a hierarchical order of Paradise which was consonant with the doctrine of love and made it possible to preserve diversity of human character in the eternal hierarchy of the kingdom of God.

The lowest, least luminous sphere, that of the moon—according to the astrological tradition cool, moist, variable and readily responding to all influences—is a kind of anteroom of Paradise; the souls that appear there, such as Piccarda and Constanza, occupy their rank not, like those of the other heavens, because of the special nature of their love, but because of a deficiency in their love; ceding to the power of others, they had been unable to fulfil their oath. The second sphere, that of Mercury, may also be interpreted as an anteroom to Paradise; the planet is a symbol of varied activity and artifice and also of the striving for fame and influence; here Dante situates those who performed good actions on earth but were too much concerned with fame and worldly interests. The next four spheres seem to represent the forms of the *caritas* of active life, the four cardinal virtues: Venus, the planet of lovers, represents temperance; the sun, where the Church Fathers and theologians appear, represents wisdom or prudence; Mars, planet of the warriors and martyrs, symbolizes fortitude; and Jupiter, planet of the princes and of the Eagle, justice. In the last planetary sphere, that of Saturn, appear the souls of the contemplative life, who devoted their lives wholly to ascetic contemplation and so achieved the form of earthly existence closest to God. Saturn is the highest rank of the ethical hierarchy in its human aspect, and there begins Dante's preparation for the divine vision of God. From there the divine ladder which Jacob saw in his dream rises up to the sublime heights of Paradise, to the Empyrean. But that is still to come. For the present Beatrice does not smile, for Dante would not yet be able to bear the sight, the heavenly choirs are silent, Dante's question about Providence cannot yet be answered, and his desire to see the soul of St. Benedict in its true, unveiled aspect cannot yet be satisfied; the privative nature of the preparation and also the cry of indignation following Peter Damian's bitter speech against the clergy, suggest something of the planet's dark, problematic character which, as other passages show, was well known to Dante.[35]

With Saturn the ethical order of the world, in so far as it involves concrete portrayal of the ultimate fate of individual souls, is concluded and the ascent begins to the true *civitas Dei* with its two hosts. After a glance back at the earth, Dante enters the heaven of fixed stars in the constellation of Gemini (the constellation of his own hour of birth). Here the triumph of Christ appears as a great sun which illumines the many thousands of stars and gathers them round it; when that symbol of the redemption of the *prima milizia,* the first host, the human race, has raised Dante's spirit above itself, he is permitted to behold Beatrice in her true aspect, and the actual presence of his youthful vision is disclosed to him as the truth revealed to man. She guides his eyes back to the host of the blessed; he is permitted to behold the coronation and ascension of Mary, who follows the already exalted Saviour. Then comes the threefold questioning of Dante, or rather, his proclamation of the spiritual fruits of redemption, of the three theological virtues: he replies to Peter concerning faith, to James concerning hope, and to John concerning love. In the crystal heaven he sees the other host of the pure Intelligences, or Angels, learns the time and nature of their creation, the concordance of their hierarchy with the heavenly and earthly order, the infinitely diverse ways in which they reflect God. But that vision too vanishes; once again he ascends: in the flowing light of the Empyrean and in the flowers on its shores he sees a symbol of the action of divine grace; in response to Beatrice's command he bends down to the glittering stream that touches the rim of his eyelids; a new degree of ecstasy comes over him, the vision changes, and in the heavenly rose, in the *convento delle bianche stole,* among the white-robed concourse,[36] the two hosts appear joined in a glory; Mary's faithful follower, St. Bernard, symbol of supreme ecstasy, intercedes with her to grant Dante the ultimate fulfillment, the vision of God; in rising illumination, impelled by will and necessity in one, his eyes penetrate deep into the light that fulfills his longing and causes his will to fuse with the movement of universal love.

In the *Paradiso* there are but few redeemed souls who appear as individual figures fraught with memories of earthly existence; and these do not, as in the other two parts of the poem, show themselves in their earlier form, so that Dante can recognize them, but are concealed in the dazzling garment of their beatitude. The higher Dante rises, the more universal and impersonal become the souls that appear; beyond Saturn, there are only the great dignitaries of the Kingdom of Heaven, whose earthly life, which prepared them for their high rank, is generally known and requires no new narrative embodiment. But he did wish to devote special treatment to two of these saints, Francis and Dominic, whose earthly lives were separated by only a century from his own and whose living action still bore a special character for him, standing out distinctly against the general background of the history of salvation. Since there was no room for such matters amid the glory of the Empyrean, where they would have had to appear, he contrives to have their lives related by other characters elsewhere. In the sphere of the sun, the Dominican St. Thomas speaks of St. Francis, while the Franciscan Bonaventure speaks of St. Dominic. Both narratives supply something that is rare in the *Comedy,* a complete biography, though a sparse one, in which Dante's goal and the saint's ultimate destination are never lost from view. There is no digression into the epic reaches of legend although, particularly in connection with St. Francis, the biographical material at Dante's disposal, with its abundance of enchanting detail, must have offered a great temptation. He sets down, almost as though drawing up a report, only what was most relevant to goal and ultimate fate, and this simple correlation of the saints' action with Dante's goal creates a compelling picture of the two saints, each with his very personal and very different ethos. They do not appear, they are merely spoken of; and it is not very different with the other figures of the planetary spheres, whose concrete reality is veiled in light. Their true, earthly figure is not seen, their only gesture is to shine with greater or lesser brightness; but their words encompass their gestures and preserve the character of the earthly man who lived in them and still lives. Often they speak very briefly but always of the crucial actions and happenings, avoiding all mere anecdote or naturalistic detail; but despite the lofty tone, the words are always very much to the point, explaining the individual's heavenly rank, connecting it with his past existence on earth, and portraying the whole man, transfigured but intact.

In the heaven of fixed stars, the heaven of the *prima milizia,* where redeemed mankind is united in the Triumph of Christ, a fourth figure joins the three examining Apostles; it is Adam, the first man, who closes the circle by relating, at the scene of its completion, the primordial beginnings of the drama. The events that he relates or explains form the starting point of the third, historico-political system of the *Comedy.*

For through Adam's fall mankind lost the original purity and goodness in which it was created and was damned like Lucifer, the fallen Angel. Eve's original sin was not the mere tasting of the forbidden fruit, but a transgressing of limits, a striving to exceed her allotted destiny: earth and heaven obeyed, only a woman who had just been created could not endure to remain within her predestined sphere. Of all created things on earth man was the most perfect: he possessed immortality, freedom, and likeness to God, but the sin of apostasy robbed him of those gifts and flung him down all the lower because he had stood so high. And man disposed of no means of reparation, for no amount of humility could fully compensate for the terrible crime of his fall away from God, the highest good; only God himself in His infinite compassion could forgive him and restore him to his former place. But God is just as well as good; justice is the eternal order of the world, and accordingly it was His pleasure to satisfy the dictates of justice even in the practice of His infinite mercy; through the incarnation of His son, born of a human mother, He engendered a pure man, who in his humility could justly and fully expunge the original sin; the union of divine and human nature in Christ is the mystery which satisfied the requirements of God's justice, for here a man by the humility of his life and Passion atoned for the original sin, but in view of the man Christ's other, divine nature, his act of atonement was an undeserved gift of God's unlimited goodness, in excess of all justice.[37]

With that idea which is known essentially to every Christian, Dante combines another which in this context may strike a modern observer as strange: it is the idea of the special mission of Rome and the Roman Empire in history. From the very beginning Divine Providence elected Rome as the capital of the world. It gave the Roman people the heroism and the spirit of self-sacrifice necessary to conquer this world and possess it in peace; and when the work of conquest and pacification, the sacred mission announced to Aeneas, was accomplished after centuries of bitter battles and sacrifices and the inhabited world lay in the hands of Augustus, the time was fulfilled and the Saviour appeared. For it was decreed that the redeemed world should abide in perfect peace, in supreme earthly perfection down to the last day; that is why Christ rendered unto Caesar the things which were Caesar's and submitted to his judgment; that is why Peter and Paul went to Rome, why Rome became the center of Christianity and the seat of the papacy. Since the very beginning of the Roman legend the two plans of Providence have been intertwined; Aeneas was granted his journey to the underworld with a view to the spiritual and secular triumph of Rome. Rome was the mirror of the divine world order, so much so that Paradise is once referred to as *quella Roma onde Christo è Romano*[38] (that Rome whereof Christ is a Roman). In the earthly Rome, as Christ made clear by his words and deeds, it was decreed that two strictly separate powers should rule in perfect balance, the spiritual power of the Pope, who must possess nothing, for his kingdom is not of this world, and the secular power of the Emperor, who is just, because God appointed him and all things earthly are in his power.

Thus the whole Roman tradition flows into the history of salvation, and the two prophecies seem complementary and almost equal in rank: Virgil's *Tu regere imperio populos* (Thou shalt rule as an empire over the nations) and the *Ave Maria*. Before the appearance of Christ, the Roman Eagle, whose deeds Justinian relates in the heaven of Mercury, was the herald, and afterward the executor, of God's plan of salvation; Tiberius the third emperor, considered as the legitimate judge over Christ the man, was the executant avenger of original sin, who satisfied God's wrath; Titus, the conqueror of Jerusalem, was the legitimate executant of vengeance against the Jews; and in the bottommost Hell, in the jaws of Lucifer, Judas has as his companions Brutus and Cassius, Caesar's murderers.[39]

But for a second time the world fell away from the divine will, and once again the sin consisted in a *trapassar del segno,* a transgressing against the earthly world order appointed by God; this sin is symbolically represented by the fate of the mystical chariot in the Earthly Paradise.[40] Christ the griffon has fastened the chariot to the tree from which Adam once plucked the forbidden fruit and which now signifies the earthly world order or the Roman empire. Beneath its branches mankind can rest in peace (Dante's sleep), and in the shadow of the tree the revealed authority of the Christian doctrine finds its natural place. The chariot of the Church resists the assaults of the Eagle (the persecutions of Christians under the first Roman emperors) and of the fox (the early Christian heretical sects); but when the Eagle covers the chariot with its wings—an allegory for the Donation of Constantine—disaster sets in. Satan rises up from the depths, breaks a piece—the spirit of humility—out of the floor of the chariot, the rest of which is filled to the brim with the Eagle's feathers (earthly goods), and the seven deadly sins appear as death's heads on the shaft and in the corners. On the seat of the chariot sits a harlot, the Roman curia, fornicating with a giant; the giant symbolizes unrestrained illegitimate power, probably in particular the French king, and in order to gain complete power over the harlot detaches the chariot from the tree and makes off with it.

The lesson of the allegory is stated clearly and passionately in many passages in the poem dealing with examples of earthly corruption. The world is out of joint, its God-ordained balance is upset, and the root of all the evil is the wealth of the Church which according to the divine order should possess nothing. Greed, the she-wolf—in a broader sense the illegitimate lust for earthly power, the striving to exceed the sphere of power appointed by God—is the worst of vices, the ruination of the world. Ever since the Roman Church with its unrestrained greed usurped even the Imperial power; ever since the Habsburg Emperors, forgetful of their duty, abandoned Italy and Rome, the head of the world—chaotic immoderation has reigned everywhere, so that everyone stretches out his hand for whatever seems within reach. The passions of men are unleashed, and the result is war and confusion. The Pope battles with Christians for earthly goods; the kings, free from the supreme sovereignty of the Emperor, rule incompetently and aimlessly; in the towns the parties struggle for a power which God has not legitimated, exploiting the cause of the Emperor or Pope for their own disgraceful ends; Church offices have become venal and their holders have taken to living in loathsome and un-Christian ostentation; disregarding their rules, the monastic orders, even the Franciscans and Dominicans, are disintegrating; disorder and corruption vie with one another, and Italy, mistress of nations, has become a brothel, a ship without helmsman in the storm.

Dante's own city of Florence occupied a special position in this world of wickedness, and not only because it was his home. It is true that his unchanged love and yearning, the bitterness of his own experience, lend a special force to his condemnation of its wickedness. But quite apart from his own motives and from his personal ties with it, Florence of all the Italian towns offered the clearest example of what Dante could not but regard as absolute evil. For it was here that the new commercial, middle-class spirit first flowered and achieved self-awareness; it was here that the great metaphysical foundations of the political world were first, in a consistently pragmatic spirit, evaluated and exploited for purely political ends; it was here that every earthly institution, regardless of its transcendent origin and authority, came to be considered, with cold calculation, as a counter in a game of forces —an attitude which became prevalent in every section of the population. And despite many setbacks that way of thinking brought Florence success even in Dante's time; trade flourished, the city increased in population and prosperity, the Florentine bankers achieved a position of European pre-eminence which was soon to be reflected, more and more conspicuously, in the political sphere. A race of worldly, calculating men arose, intent on profit and power, to whom the bonds of the traditional world order meant nothing, even though for business reasons they paid it lip service when possible; and when a new culture arose among them, it was no longer an ecumenical wisdom authorized by God, which permeates and regulates all earthly life, but an aesthetic hedonism utterly devoid of moral obligation. Party strife with all its vicissitudes and turmoil brought the city more profit than harm; for it promoted the free play of forces and with it the process of selection by which an organism preserves its youth and is enabled to adapt itself at every moment to the shifting demands of practical life, to assimilate and master them. That is the idea which is expressed only half consciously in the often cited passage of Machiavelli, where he says that nothing more clearly indicates the inner strength of the city of Florence than the greatness it has achieved despite the terrible party strife that would have been the downfall of any other state.[41] But Machiavelli was too much inclined to regard the city's intestine struggles as a mere obstacle that had been overcome; actually the obstacle was productive, and when he goes on to say that the city would have achieved incomparably greater flowering if it had preserved inner unity from the start, we believe him to be mistaken; Florence, *fior che sempre rinovella*,[42] flower forever renewed, grew great by its inner struggles.

Dante wanted none of it. He would never have recognized a political life based on autonomous earthly success; the earthly world lies in the hands of God; only those who draw legitimacy from God are entitled to possess its goods, and then only to the extent provided for by the legitimation. A struggle for earthly goods is a trespass against the divine will; it signifies anti-Christian confusion, and even on the practical plane it can lead only to disaster, to secular and eternal ruin. It never occurred to him as he deplored and condemned the disunity, the struggles and calamities of his time, that they might be preparing the way for a new, immanent but fruitful order of life. Nowhere does the poet strike a modern observer as so alien and reactionary, so unprophetic and blind to the future. But when we consider with what sacrifices that future, the culture of the new era, was bought, how the schism between inner and outward life became more and more painful, how the political and human unity of life was lost, how the fragmentation and inefficacy of all ideologies became evident to everyone, even in the lowest stations; when, further, we bear in mind that all modern attempts to restore a human community have rested on foundations far shakier than those of Dante's world order—we shall not, to be sure, cherish any futile, absurd desire to revive what is irretrievably lost, but neither shall we be tempted to despise or condemn the meaningful order on which Dante's thinking was based.

As we have seen, the source and at the same time the most glaring sign of political evil was for Dante the temporal expansion of the Holy See. Free from the Imperial power, it became untrue to its mission and drew all Christendom with it into perdition. And yet, though Dante went so far in his attack on the Curia as to liken it to the Babylonian harlot, he did not question its authority. Strange as it may seem, he looked upon even the most depraved of Popes as a *successor Petri,* vicar of Christ on earth, endowed with the power to loose and to bind: "Ye have the Old and the New Testament," says Beatrice, "and the shepherd of the Church to guide you; let this suffice you, unto your salvation."[43] It would never have occurred to Dante to extend his opposition to the Curia to the realm of faith. Dante and others of his day could well be horrified at the thought that a man, whose soul has been relegated to the lowest reaches of Hell, should have been the legitimate vicar of Christ on earth, legitimately wielding the highest power, but they saw nothing impossible or absurd in it.

We know that Dante's political hopes revived once again when the Emperor Henry VII came down from Luxemburg on his Italian campaign, and that Dante supported him by word and perhaps by deed. Henry's failures and death did not discourage him. Henry VII is the one figure in the history of his own time whom Dante expressly situates in the Empyrean: Beatrice shows him the throne destined for the Emperor's soul, the soul "of the lofty Henry who shall come to straighten Italy ere she be ready for it."[44] Italy was not yet ready; but one day the sacred order would be restored on earth. That was Dante's passionate faith, and he professed it in dark, fantastic prophesies, which have never ceased to arouse the interest of posterity and the zeal of the exegete, though in six centuries no one has found an altogether reliable interpretation of them.

There are two main prophecies: the one is uttered by Virgil[45] after Dante shrinks back in horror from the wolf of covetousness; this ever hungry beast, says Virgil, will be the ruin of many until the greyhound, the *Veltro,* comes to slay it, saving unhappy Italy and chasing the she-wolf back into Hell, whence Satan's envy turned her loose upon the earth. In the other passage,[46] it is Beatrice who speaks; the allegory of the chariot, that we have described above, is at an end, the giant has gone off with the harlot enthroned upon the chariot of the Church; Beatrice utters the glad prophecy from the Gospel of St. John (16:16): *Modicum, et non videbitis me . . .* (A little while, and ye shall not see me . . .); then she prophesies the salvation of the Church: the Eagle will not always be without heirs; already the constellation is near under which the *cinquecento dieci e cinque* (the five hundred ten and five) sent by God will slay the giant and the harlot.

It seems obvious that those two prophecies, in which Reason and Revelation speak of future things on earth, are related, that the first is contained in the second which completes and clarifies it; and indeed, no one has ever seriously denied the connection between them. It is also quite clear what is meant in both passages by the present evil that the future savior will slay: the she-wolf and the harlot are symbols for the sin of covetousness which has taken hold of the spiritual leader of the world, the papacy, and hence also for the papacy itself. Many passages in the poem make it clear that the papal usurpation of temporal goods is the source of all earthly confusion; the image of the shepherd turned into a wolf by the *maledetto fiore,* the accursed flower, that is, Florentine gold, which is leading Christendom to perdition, recurs in many variations. Dante's own lot, the many diatribes in the *Comedy,* particularly St. Peter's vehement words in the heaven of the fixed stars, the whole texture of Dante's political theories—all that makes so clear who it was he regarded as the true obstacle to earthly beatitude, that any other interpretation seems strained. We can also arrive, with some degree of certainty, at a general idea of who the expected savior is. For what is lacking in the world? Imperial sovereignty: the Eagle is without heirs, the German Albrecht forsakes his empire, Henry comes too soon: but Rome, the head of the Christian world, requires two suns to illumine both paths, the earthly and the heavenly; now, however, one has extinguished the other, the sword has merged with the pastoral staff, and the right order has been destroyed by violence; the earth lacks a legitimate ruler, and that is why the *humana famiglia,* the human community, is going astray. To me there seems no doubt, and it is the prevailing opinion, that the savior can only be a bearer of the Imperial power; but from the symbols and chronological specifications that Dante adds,[47] I can derive no definite information; only one thing is stated clearly, namely, that Italy above all must be saved, whence it follows that the mission of Rome as sovereign of the world remains as valid for the future as for the past.

But those historico-political symbols are rooted in much deeper layers of ancient mythical faith. For the first, the Virgilian prophecy, is given at the foot of a sunlit mountain, which is the "beginning and ground of all joy," after Dante has tried in vain to climb it by his own strength; the second is uttered on the summit of Purgatorio, in the Earthly Paradise. But the mountain of Purgatory, inaccessible in the ocean of the southern hemisphere, with its seven terraces, with the Garden of Eden and the miraculous tree, is the element of Dante's cosmology which is most deeply rooted in the world-renewal mysticism of the Near East. It points back to the seven terraces of the tower of Babylon, mountain of the gods and symbol of the planetary spheres, to Ezechiel's mountain of God, to the seven gates of the Gnostic journey of the soul, with the seven spheres of purification, each watched over by an archon (after passing the last sphere, that of fire, the soul is privileged to partake of the marriage feast of Christ and Sophia); to Cabalist, Joachimite, and Franciscan myths of world renewal. Dante is borne upward to the first gate by the ambiguous figure of Lucia-Aquila—an anagram—who at the very beginning of the poem has acquainted Virgil with the mission of Beatrice and in whose person the symbol of illuminating grace, *gratia illuminans,* seems to be combined with that of the right world order, the Roman Empire; at the summit of the mountain he is received by Matelda, unquestionably a symbol of pure and active life amid still uncorrupted nature, who leads him to his bath in Lethe and Eunoe, to purifying oblivion and new birth; and here too he beholds the mystical procession with the chariot bearing the transfigured Beatrice. Thus if Dante's journey to the Other World signifies the preparatory way of purification and the rebirth of the individual soul through the immediate *visio Dei*—then the prophecies at the beginning and end of the journey, concerning the future of the human community, can only refer to the future rebirth of all humankind and to the future Golden Age: the age when not only the heavenly kingdom but the earthly kingdom as well will be perfect and immaculate in accordance with its God-ordained destiny, when the Earthly Paradise will be realized on earth. I cannot make up my mind whether to accept the theory that *Il Veltro* is a composite of the Veronese Cangrande with the Grand Khan of the Tartars—from the land of felt (*veltro*) huts and blankets—or the notion (which strikes me as more likely) that the *cinquecento dieci e cinque* is an allusion to the Age of the Phoenix—but one thing that stands out compellingly in the works of the Germans who have formulated such theories— Bassermann, Kampers, and Burdach[48]—is the important part played by the world-renewal myths of the Near East in Dante's work. It is not easy to prove that Dante drew directly on any particular source, and so far no one has succeeded in doing so; however, it does not seem unlikely that certain of his sources were little known at his time, for otherwise his sons and the other commentators of the next generation would surely have had something more definite to say about some of the more puzzling passages. In Dante innumerable myths of rebirth (and the same is true of many other traditions and currents of thought) flow together and take on new force and vitality. And indeed it is only in his work, ordered and embedded in the hierarchically balanced system of his vision, that they have retained the measure and dignity they deserve. As they appear in Dante, they are neither the extravagant outpourings of an irresponsible fantasy nor impatient makeshift utopias.

The hierarchical structure of the historico-political world order is not set forth in the *Comedy* with the same clear continuity as the physical or ethical order; it is difficult, for example, to maintain that each stage in the journey symbolizes a particular stage of social life, and the attempts to demonstrate a concordance of that kind—Fritz Kern in his *Humana Civilitas*[49] has offered a highly instructive and well thought-out attempt of the sort—strike me as exceedingly far-fetched. Nevertheless, when we consider the *Comedy* in that light, our attention is drawn to an image which calls for such an interpretation. It is the antithesis of the two cities: Dis the *civitas diaboli* in the *Inferno*, and in the *Paradiso* the *civitas Dei*. The walled city of Lucifer, whose gates are closed to the wise poet of the Roman world order, so that a divine messenger, perhaps *Il Veltro*, must force admittance, is the realm of *malizia* (wickedness) and the aim of wickedness is injustice. And injustice is not only a sin against God, but also an offense against one's neighbor and against the right life on earth; the city of Dis is the abode of social perdition. It is represented, to be sure, as part of the total divine order which includes evil, and in that sense it is well ordered; but it persists in impotent rebellion against the high power of God, for their evil will has deprived its inhabitants of sound insight and hence of freedom; of the freedom, which men possess in their earthly life, to choose the right course. Consequently, they can will only evil, and they consume themselves in the hopeless corruption of hatred and blindness. They cannot perform any fruitful work in common, for the evil will, though common to them all, does not bind but confuses and isolates; the perverted will that dominates each one, is directed against his fellow in perdition. The community is hopelessly enmeshed in war and misery; though powerless to act, Lucifer, its king, is still strong enough to blow the icy petrifying breath of hatred over his country; through the center of it,[50] in the circle where the violent against God suffer the rain of fire, Phlegethon, the river of seething blood, flows in its hard stony bed; it is a part of the river of Hell, formed by the tears of the Old Man of Crete, his back to the East and his eyes turned toward Rome as though peering into a mirror, who symbolizes the gradual decline through the ages of the human race forsaken by grace.

By contrast, the *civitas Dei* in Paradise is a land of justice; here dwell the souls in their proper order, working in common, each delighting in its rank, partaking of a true good, which is inexhaustible in supply and confers ever increasing enjoyment as more redeemed souls have a share in it. In the manifestations of the blessed in the planetary spheres, the diversity of dispositions and vocations[51] forms the natural order within which man becomes a citizen;[52] in the measure of his aptitudes he becomes a member of the human community whose aim is the actualization of the divine order on earth, and it is that human community which in the course of an upright life leads him to sound insight and beatitude; and thus he becomes a citizen of the kingdom of God, the true *Roma aeterna,* occupying the rung of the hierarchy befitting his predisposition.

Between the two cities lies the mountain of Purgatory; it is not only a place of penance, for here also the souls practice living in common and are trained in the exercise of true freedom. In ante-Purgatory, the waiting souls, still unable to rise by their own power, require outward guidance and help; Cato, the righteous fighter for earthly freedom, sternly shows them the way when sensual pleasure threatens to turn them aside, and the angels with the two swords protect the defenseless souls from temptation. Once the souls have passed through the gate of Purgatory proper, an independent will awakens in them, a striving for purification in common; first they atone for the grave vices which endanger the life of the community, then for the less serious sensual disorders which hamper their ethical freedom and hence the social order chiefly when they are carried to excess. The last purification in the fire of the seventh circle confers freedom: in crowning Dante sovereign over himself,[53] Virgil frees him from all authority. Liberated, Dante enters the Earthly Paradise, where man lives in the midst of peaceful nature in a state of innocence, needful of no master; but this is only a place of transition, a *status viatoris,* for even the most perfect earthly life is not the ultimate purpose of the human community, but preparation for the sight of God, which means eternal beatitude.

As we see, this order is perfectly consonant with the two others, for the whole poem, whether considered from a physical, an ethical, or a historico-political point of view, builds up the destiny of man and his soul and sets it before us in a concrete image: God and creation, spirit and nature lie enclosed and ordered in perfect necessity (which however is nothing other than perfect freedom allotted to each thing according to its essence). Nothing is left open but the narrow cleft of earthly human history, the span of man's life on earth, in which the great and dramatic decision must fall; or to look at it the other way round, from the standpoint of human life, this life, in all the diversity of its manifestations, is measured by its highest goal, where individuality achieves actual fulfillment and all society finds its predestined and final resting place in the universal order. Thus, even though the *Comedy* describes the state of souls after death, its subject, in the last analysis, remains earthly life with its entire range and content; everything that happens below the earth or in the heavens above relates to the human drama in this world. But since the human world receives the measures by which it is to be molded and judged from the other world, it is neither a realm of dark necessity nor a peaceful land of God; no, the cleft is really open, the span of life is short, uncertain, and decisive for all eternity; it is the magnificent and terrible gift of potential freedom which creates the urgent, restless, human, and Christian-European atmosphere of the irretrievable, fleeting moment that must be taken advantage of; God's grace is infinite, but so also is His justice and one does not negate the other. The hearer or reader enters into the narrative; in the great realm of fulfilled destiny he sees only himself alone unfulfilled, still acting upon the real, decisive stage, illumined from above but still in the dark; he is in danger, the decision is near, and in the images of Dante's pilgrimage that draw before him he sees himself damned, making atonement, or saved, but always himself, not extinguished, but eternal in his very own essence.

Thus in truth the *Comedy* is a picture of earthly life. The human world in all its breadth and depth is gathered into the structure of the hereafter and there it stands: complete, unfalsified, yet encompassed in an eternal order; the confusion of earthly affairs is not concealed or attenuated or immaterialized, but preserved in full evidence and grounded in a plan which embraces it and raises it above all contingency. Doctrine and fantasy, history and myth are woven into an almost inextricable skein; often an almost unconscionable amount of time and effort is required to fathom the content of a single line; but once one has succeeded in surveying the whole, the hundred cantos, with their radiant *terza rima,* their perpetual binding and loosing, reveal the dreamlike lightness and remoteness of a perfection that seems to hover over us like a dance of unearthly figures. Yet the law of that dream is a human reason operating according to a plan and conscious of its destiny, which it is able to govern and order because its courageous good will has been favored by divine grace.

V

THE PRESENTATION

Thus we find in the *Comedy* an image of the earthly world in all its diversity, transposed into the world of ultimate destiny and perfect order. And now that we have spoken in the most general terms of its content and structure we shall try to show how they are reflected in the particular scenes and images.

Dante journeys through the Other World and there, in the stations which mark their ultimate destiny, he encounters the souls of men he has known or with whose lives he is familiar. Even one who knows nothing of the *Comedy* can, by reflecting on the situation, easily imagine the emotion aroused by those meetings and the natural occasion they offer for the most authentic, most powerful, and most human expression. The encounters do not take place in this life, where men are always met with in a state of contingency that manifests only a part of their essence, and where the very intensity of life in the most vital moments makes self-awareness difficult and renders a true encounter almost impossible. Nor do they take place in a hereafter where what is most personal in the personality is effaced by the shadows of death and nothing remains but a feeble, veiled, or indifferent recollection of life. No, the souls of Dante's other world are not dead men, they are the truly living; though the concrete data of their lives and the atmosphere of their personalities are drawn from their former existences on earth, they manifest them here with a completeness, a concentration, an actuality, which they seldom achieved during their term on earth and assuredly never revealed to anyone else. And so it is that Dante finds them; surprise, astonishment, joy, or horror grips both parties to the meeting, for the dweller in the Other World as he is shown there is also deeply moved by an encounter with one of the living; the mere fact of seeing and recognizing one another reaches into the deepest foundations of human feeling and creates images of unparalleled poetic force and richness.

Thus the meetings between souls in the *Comedy* offer a number of scenes which, though they derive the elements of their expression from the memory of earthly encounters, far surpass any possible earthly encounter by the degree of emotion that accompanies them and the wealth of situations they disclose. They are most moving where Dante was bound to the other by earthly ties, either of actual life together or of inner, spiritual influence. The passion which, either from diffidence or from lack of occasion to speak, tends in temporal existence to hide, bursts forth here, all in one piece, as though moved by the awareness that this is its one and only opportunity to express itself.

In Dante's extreme need in the face of impending ruin, the helper sent by divine grace appears before him: and it is Virgil! But even before he has recognized him, Dante's distress impels him to throw the whole of himself into his cry of supplication; and when the master of his art and precursor of his thinking makes himself known, Dante's love and admiration spring forth naturally and uncontrollably, and in his situation the constitutive words, which provide the essential picture both of the other and of himself, seem quite self-evident, words full of pathos, yet genuinely rooted in the specific occasion. And when in the triumphal procession in the Earthly Paradise Beatrice appears; when Dante, in need of help, turns to Virgil to say: "Less than a dram of blood is left in me that trembleth not" and no longer finds the *dolcissimo padre* at his side; and when the name of Dante rings out like a call at the Last Judgment, the well-prepared emotion, grounded in his past and present fate, legitimated no less by reason than by the heart, the emotion which is true readiness to know and acknowledge himself, grips us scarcely less than it does him, so that the reader too might well say in

Dante's words: *men che dramma di sangue m'è rimaso che non tremi.*

In these two special cases the emotion strikes only the one partner to the meeting, Dante: for the two others, Virgil and Beatrice, know in advance whom they are to encounter, they have received their mission from above and are from another sphere. But everywhere else the encounter grips both participants in it with equal force. To the same category—the meeting with a former mentor or model—belongs the scene with Brunetto Latini,[1] which remains engraved in the memory of every reader of the *Inferno*. From the raised dike on which he is advancing Dante is unable to recognize the Sodomites peering up at him through the darkness from the burning desert, until one of them plucks him by the skirt and calls: "What a wonder!" "And I, when he stretched out his arm to me, fixed my eyes on his baked aspect, so that the scorching of his visage hindered not my mind from knowing him; and bending my face to his, I answered: *'Siete voi qui, ser Brunetto?'* ('Are you here, Ser Brunetto?') And he: *'O figliuol mio . . .'* ('O my son . . .')." And yet that picture, which introduces and justifies Brunetto's significant words, seems only a sketch, a foretaste of a later image which fully develops the feeling implicit in the theme here suggested, namely, the meeting between Statius and Virgil.[2] There for the first time Dante develops all the wealth of possibilities offered by the subject and locale of the *Comedy* and employs them in connection with the same theme, the encounter between a spiritual father and his pupil. Those two men were not contemporaries; they did not know one another; twelve centuries had passed since they lived; Virgil dwelt in Limbo with the pagans; Statius, according to Dante's fiction a secret Christian, made atonement in Purgatory. At the very hour when Virgil is leading his pupil Dante through Purgatory, Statius attains the end of his term of purification; he feels free and ready to ascend to heaven; an earthquake announces the redemption of a soul; he begins his ascent; the two pilgrims are joined by the still unrecognized third, who does not know whom he has before him. He informs them of his life and poetic work and concludes with the praise of Virgil: the *Aeneid* was his nurse, without it he could have accomplished

136

nothing; to have lived when Virgil lived, he would gladly have awaited his liberation for another year in Purgatory. At those words Virgil turns to Dante and beckons him to be silent: but the power of the will has its limits . . . "I did but smile, like one who makes a sign; at that the shade was silent and looked me in the eyes. . . . And he said: 'So may your great toil achieve its end, why did your face but now display to me a flash of laughter?' Now I am caught on either side; one makes me keep silence, the other conjures me to speak; therefore I sigh and am understood by my master, and he said to me, 'Have no fear of speaking. . . .' Therefore I: 'Perhaps you marvel, O ancient spirit, at the laugh I gave, but I desire that even greater wonder seize you. He who guides my eyes on high, is Virgil. . . .' Already he was stooping to embrace my Teacher's feet; but he said: 'Brother, do not so, for you are a shade and a shade you see.' And he, rising: 'Now can you comprehend the measure of the love that warms me toward you, when I forget our nothingness, and treat shades as a solid thing.'"

Less grandiose of gesture, but permeated with the sweet memory of the old life together are the meetings between friends. Among the emaciated gluttons in Purgatory (Canto 23), Dante meets Forese Donati, the friend of his youth with whom he had carried on a sparklingly irreverent controversy in sonnets: "from the hollow of the head a shade turned its eyes to me and fixedly did gaze; then cried aloud. . . . Never had I recognized him by the face, but in his voice was revealed to me that which was blotted out in his countenance. This spark rekindled within me all my knowledge of the changed features, and I recognized the face of Forese." *E ravvisai la faccia di Forese!* The power implicit in such a meeting—in such a place—becomes evident when we note how this last line is the culmination of an inner movement built up step by step, while the ensuing dialogue follows from the contrast between Forese's sunken features and his radiant, exuberant youth. Dante had known Charles Martell of Anjou, the young king of Hungary, in Florence in 1294; the king was then in his early twenties and died soon thereafter. Now he meets him in the heavenly sphere of Venus,[3] swathed in beatitude like a silkworm in its cocoon and thus unrecognizable: he greets

Dante with the most beautiful verses of Dante's youth, so disclosing his identity as well as his love for Dante, and the memory of his youthful admiration and devotion shines forth amid the beatitude of the third sphere. Dante does not meet Guido Cavalcanti, for during part of 1300 Guido was still alive, but finds his father among the heretics lying in red-hot sarcophagi.[4] Cavalcanti sits up to see whether his son is not there too, for it seems to the older man that Guido's mind was profound enough to enable him, just as well as his friend Dante, to enter the underworld in his lifetime; but at a word from which he gathers that his son is now no longer among the living, he sinks back lamenting, an image of paternal pride and haughty Epicureanism, for this too is implied in his insistence on *altezza d'ingegno* (on the height of genius), his praise of the sweet light of the sun, and his indifference to Guido's ultimate fate, about which he does not even inquire. The scene is an interruption of Dante's meeting with the Ghibelline leader Farinata degli Uberti, one of the finest among the long series of meetings with his compatriots. In Dante's hereafter, common birthplace and language provide a bond of love and joy, and in the *Comedy* the motif of the compatriot encountered far from home, which may strike us as sentimental, is varied and raised to sublime heights. Engaged in conversation, Virgil and Dante pass by the tombs of the heretics, and Farinata recognizes Dante as a Florentine by his manner of speech; suddenly Dante is terrified by a voice issuing from one of the tombs: *"O Tosco che per la città del foco vivo ten vai così parlando onesto . . ."* ("O Tuscan! who through the city of fire goest alive, speaking thus decorously").[5] The sentence itself is a magnificent example of lofty speech; consummately modelled down to the very last syllable, it frames a complex thought in the simplest and most direct words; if we say it over a few times, it will bring home to us all the intensity of the great Farinata's emotion and the power beneath which his words conceal their richness; but what Farinata himself means by the *parlare onesto* (decorous speech) is the beautiful Florentine dialect, and so we learn from this passage that Dante speaks Tuscan in discoursing with Virgil, just as Virgil as a Mantuan— as is shown by another, very similar passage[6]—employs the

Lombard Italian of the year 1300. In another connection we shall have more to say of this passage, which also contains an adjuration by the common homeland. In regard to our present theme, the encounter with a countryman, we have another Mantuan at our disposal: that is Sordello, the Provençal poet from Mantua, who at nightfall in Ante-Purgatory,[7] solitary and aloof as a resting lion, scarcely wishes to answer Virgil's question until the word Mantua makes him start up: *"O Mantovano, io son Sordello de la tua terra—e l'un l'altro abbracciava"* ("O Mantuan, I am Sordello of your city.—And one embraced the other."). There is no better example of the power of the setting which makes such meetings possible; for without the introduction and the occasion it so naturally offers, the ensuing apostrophe to Italy and the Emperor would be mere rhetoric, while, placed as it is, it becomes, with all the strict clarity of its thinking, a cry uttered in a real situation; Dante and the listener, the one creating, the other receiving, are equally prepared to savor the passion that now bursts forth, and yet it is not a product of artifice, but with all its artfulness wholly natural, because it corresponds to the natural movement of human feeling.

With that we conclude our list of encounters, for to exhaust them we should have to copy out a large part of the poem, and we hope we have made it sufficiently clear what they communicate: namely, the state of agitation in which the souls are met, partly because of the place itself and partly because of the presence of a living man in it. Not all are glad of the meeting, for in the lower circles of Hell there are some who would have preferred to remain unrecognized; and not all those who are glad are glad in the same way; the passionate longing of the lower spirits for news of the world, their eagerness to know whether they are remembered on earth, are diminished in Purgatory, mingled with other, more Christian motives for rejoicing; while in Paradise the source of the soul's rejoicing is the love they are able to bestow on the favored guest. But all who are gathered in the Other World, men of all times and countries, with all their wisdom and folly, good and evil, love and hatred of the world, the whole epitome of history—all of them find in the living Dante, who comes to them, an occasion and a need to state what they are and to explain in clear and tangible terms how they came to their ultimate destination.

It is not always easy for them to say what they wish to. Particularly in the *Inferno,* but also in the *Purgatorio,* there seems to be a barrier between their need to communicate and its satisfaction—and that barrier, created by their situation of punishment or atonement, makes their communication all the more poignant when it does break forth. Those men with their terribly disfigured or tormented bodies, some in eternal motion, others in painful immobility, have scarcely strength or time to speak. Yet they wish to speak and must speak; they express themselves painfully and laboriously, and it is their torment and effort that give their words and gestures such compelling power. Wrapped in flames, the elder Montefeltro approaches the two pilgrims;[8] slowly and painfully his words make their way through the roaring flame, and full of fear that his listeners may lose patience, he beseeches them to remain and speak with their countryman; until at length the question toward which he is aiming, and which has filled his heart all the while, bursts forth like an explosion of his whole physical and spiritual being: *"Dimmi se i Romagnuoli han pace or guerra"* ("Tell me if the Romagnuols have peace or war"). We have designedly chosen this example precisely because the sentence that crowns the scene is not in itself so significant, for what is more natural than that a dead man, who once played an important part in the destinies of his native place, should ask what is going on there now? But the particular qualities of the setting where the question is asked and here in particular the barrier the speaker must surmount in order to utter it, charge the question itself with all the questioner's yearning and feverish curiosity.

Thus far we have tried to show that the souls encountered in the Other World are of necessity ready and willing to reveal their innermost reality and that the power of their utterance is sometimes further enhanced by the difficulties that stand in its way. But we have not yet considered their "innermost reality" as such, nor have we inquired where Dante derived its constitutive elements. A very general answer suggests itself without difficulty: he took them from his own experience as he remembered it; and in selecting and blending his memories, he employed a definite method of synopsis or abstraction. Thus all the figures of his great poem are derived from Dante's own inner being: that much is obvious and requires no further discussion; the material with which he worked was an almost superhuman fund of experience and a divinatory gift which enabled him to fathom all varieties and degrees of human feeling. Far more difficult is the question of selection, for in each case he had to choose from among a superabundance of traits and interpretations, and the true reality distilled by such selection hinges on the authority Dante invokes. For what he represents is not the whole epic breadth of life, but a single moment of reality; and that single moment, moreover, encompasses a man's ultimate fate as determined by Providence. Thus when Dante has his figures appear in this or that part of the Other World, he not only purports to represent their true essence, but also to know God's judgment upon them or rather to have beheld it in a vision: an absurd and presumptuous falsehood unless the vision is the evident truth; unless it accords with the reader's profoundest convictions and at the same time rises above them, synthesizing disparities and creatively revealing a common element on which the synthesis is based.

All that enters into the synopsis or abstraction by which, as we have said, Dante solved his problem of selection. He does not relate the whole life, he does not spread out the whole soul and analyze it in all its parts; he omits many things. In one of his titles, Rabelais calls himself an *abstracteur de quinte essence* (an abstractor of quintessence); a modern painter is quoted as saying that painting is omission; Dante seems to proceed somewhat in that way. But our comparisons are taken from more recent times: did any poet work in a similar way before Dante? Apparently not; when the ancient and medieval poets wished to set forth a character's whole personality, they drew the essence from the whole epic breadth of his life; when they gave only an excerpt of the life, it meant that they had no thought of portraying the whole man; in considering a lover, a jealous man, a glutton, or a nuisance, they did not concern themselves in the least with anything else he might be other than loving, jealous, gluttonous, or importunate. Even the classical tragedy, which may be said to "omit" a good deal and yet to aim at the whole of the man, requires an event which unfolds in time; on the basis of this event, the tragic poet decides what is to be included and what omitted, and it is through the event that the hero replies, more and more clearly and in the end definitively, to the question put to him by his destiny, to the question of who he really is. But Dante records no events; he has only a moment in which everything must be revealed; a very special moment, to be sure, for it is eternity. And he gives us something which the Greek tragedy scorned, namely, the individual, concrete qualities of man: through language, tone, gesture, bearing, he penetrates to the essence. The reader of a Greek tragedy, it is true, can form a concrete picture of Prometheus or Antigone or Hippolytus, and the Greek spectator could do so in still higher degree; but the portrayal left far more room for the viewer's imagination than in Dante's poem, where every accent and every gesture are exactly defined.

In this connection it would be interesting to observe how unity of body and soul had become more intense and taken on new meaning since the individual human body, through Christian dogma, had come to partake of eternity. But that would take us too far afield. Instead let us see what it is that Dante omits. This is made clear by our comparison with earlier poets: he omits temporal events. In the hereafter there is no more temporal happening: history is at an end, replaced by memory. Nothing new will ever again happen to the souls except on the Day of Judgment, which will merely bring about an intensification of their present state. They have cast off their *status viatoris* (their wayfarer's state) and entered into the *status recipientis pro meritis* (the state of those rewarded according to merit), and with nonessential reservations that is also true of the souls in Purgatory. No longer is there any hope or fear of change, there is no uncertain future to give the souls consciousness of the dimension of time. Nothing happens to them any longer, or rather, what happens to them will keep happening forever. But that situation without time or history is the fruit of their history on earth, and in thinking and speaking of themselves, they are constrained to see both in one. Among their innumerable experiences, their memory necessarily chooses those which were decisive, and that is the very essence of their memory; for God by His judgment has shown them what was decisive. Thus history with its vicissitudes has been taken from them and what remains is a memory which infallibly strikes the essential. In addition the souls have retained their individual form; however, it is not their changing historical form, influenced by the changing historical situation, but a definitive, true and authentic form, which God's judgment has disclosed and, as it were, fixated for all eternity. In the *Inferno,* to be sure, certain figures, the suicides for instance, have suffered significant changes, and others like the thieves incur continuous change; but in those cases it must be assumed that metamorphosis is their eternal form and represents—if I may use a hazardous expression—the concrete sum of their earthly existence. And with slight modifications all that is equally applicable to the souls in Purgatory; to them too, a decisive and ultimate fate has been meted out, and they too must relate it to the memory of their life on earth; their form, to be sure, is not final, and yet it is, in so far as it symbolizes the sum of their former being, and in so far as it will change only at a time and in a way that have already been determined. True, they do not yet know when that will happen; they still possess hope and expectation, and in this respect the Mountain of Purgatory retains some of the historical character of the *status viatoris;* but their uncertainty is very slight compared to the uncertainty of earthly life; there is no earthly experience in Purgatory, but only the memory of such experience.

And so temporal events are eliminated, only memory is preserved, and it is only by way of memory that reality enters into the Other World, and yet, in the last analysis, memory, from which all chance and every contingent relation to a temporal situation on earth is removed, captures the essence not only with greater intellectual precision but also more concretely and completely than do temporal events with their uncertainty and ambiguity. In the hereafter, men have self-knowledge, for it has been conferred upon them by God's judgment. And self-knowledge, even the fragmentary, ambiguous self-knowledge which we mortals possess on earth, is made possible only by memory. To be sure, the potential simultaneity of all events in memory is always actualized in a definite image; but the image itself is shaped by a consciousness whose whole experience has contributed to the shaping; the moment of the event, by contrast, is obscure; though others may understand us at this moment, we cannot understand ourselves. Thus in making his characters' self-portrayal flow from their memory, Dante brings out their innermost experience; they recollect, and the object or substance of their recollection is given them by their ultimate fate, which shows them its full concordance with their essence. Consequently they cannot help remembering the essential, and whatever the particular image which memory may conjure up from their days on earth, it must always be exhaustive and decisive in respect of their essence; even those who would gladly conceal their innermost being are compelled to speak by their encounter with the living man,[9] and the expression they find must be the sharpest and most personal expression, for they know themselves and the meaning of their lives and in their supreme actuality have remained identical with themselves.

Thus the poem consists of a long series of self-portraits, which are so clear and complete that concerning those men, who have long been dead and who lived under such very different conditions from ourselves or who perhaps never lived at all, we know something which often remains hidden from us in our thoughts about ourselves or those with whom we are in daily contact: namely, the simple meaning which dominates and orders their whole existence. The meaning that Dante gives us is for the most part very simple, often stated in a short sentence; but even when it is so simple as to seem almost threadbare, a well-nigh superhuman penetration was required to find it, and it gains its richness from the abundance of events which surround it and from which it is distilled; only a small part of the man's experience is expressed, but that small part is the essential, what is omitted is present in it by implication. When the elder Montefeltro says: *"Io fui uom d'arme, e poi fui cordigliero"*[10] ("I was a man of arms and then became a Cordelier"), Dante has put his finger on the essential character of that hard, crafty man with his secret but insufficient yearning for purity; and when of all the episodes of his life only a single one is related, the story of how he could not resist the temptation to exercise his often tested guile one last time, that one event not only determines his ultimate fate but also characterizes the man, and all the rest of his life that remains unexpressed—the struggles, the hardships, the intrigues, and the days of vain repentance—is implicit in the characterization.

No imitation of present events can be more real and penetrating than memory in Dante's Other World. Let us consider the theme of the frail young woman whose husband has her secretly murdered in a desert place; let us attempt a dramatic or epic treatment of the theme, enriched with all the motives and atmospheric details which it admits of; and then read the last two tercets of the Ante-Purgatory, in which Pia de' Tolomei, last among those who have met a violent death, raises her voice:

> "Deh, quando tu sarai tornato al mondo,
> E risposato de la lunga via,"
> Seguitò il terzo spirito al secondo,
> "Ricorditi di me che son la Pia:
> Siena mi fè; disfecemi Maremma;
> Salsi colui che innanellata pria
> Disposando m'avea con la sua gemma."[11]

"Pray, when you shall return to the world, and are rested from your long journey," followed the third spirit after the second.

"Remember me, who am La Pia: Siena made me, Maremma unmade me: 'tis known to him who, first plighting troth, had wedded me with his gem."

Here no motivation or detail is given; Dante's contemporaries may well have filled out the allusion, but we ourselves have no definite information about Pia de' Tolomei. Yet nothing seems lacking; she is entirely real and distinct. Her memory is wholly concentrated on the hour of her death, which sealed her final fate; in that memory and in her supplication to remember her on earth, the whole of her being unfolds; and the one line that is not concerned with herself, her sweet and tender words to Dante —"e riposato de la lunga via"—tells us all we need to know of this woman in order to perceive her life in its full actuality.

This quintessence of character, arrived at by self-recollection in the predestined place of ultimate destiny, seldom has its source in what moderns would call the "atmosphere" or "milieu." Almost always memory is directed toward a definite act or event, and it is from this act or event that the character's aura arises. The act, the event, the vice or virtue, the pragmatic historical situation—in short, a decisive concrete fact—suffices to manifest the man connected with it in all his sensuous reality; there are no everyday naturalistic particulars. When one of the souls being scourged in hell, who wished at first to hide, merely says: *"Io fui colui che la Ghisolabella condussi a far la voglia del Marchese"*[12] ("It was I who led the fair Ghisola to do the Marquis' will"), he has no need to recount the details of his former life; in such a place these words suffice. Herein Dante proceeds in the manner of legend or myth, whose poetic characters or concrete figures are always based on tangible data. His method differs not only from that of the later naturalistic poets, who present the character in his social relations, habits, and environment before letting him act, but also from that of the ancient poets, who treated the legends and myths in a tragic or epic manner; for the ancient poets had nothing essential to invent, the characters and fates were there, known to every reader or member of the audience. Dante, however, created his own myths; though the persons and destinies he treated may have been known to many contemporaries, they were in large part subject to varying interpretation and thus unformed before Dante took them up. In his use of known but not yet mythically shaped persons, Dante shows most resemblance to the old Attic comedy, to the plays of Aristophanes, who also liked to lift earthly characters into another realm, where they revealed themselves. Vico saw a connection between the title of Dante's poem and ancient comedy, though he found no basis for supposing the association to be anything more than playful wit.[13] Be that as it may, the presence of contemporaries and critique of the times exhaust the resemblance, for Aristophanes does not mold his figures into a definitive mythical or ideal type, as Dante does in his poem. Dante's naturalism is something new: the directness with which he lifts one among the multitude of his contemporaries into the Other World, there to interpret his essential reality, as though he were as famous as a mythical, or at least historically established figure whose significance is known to all—that directness seems to have been unknown before him. It will be worth our while to illustrate the point by an example. An ancient, for example, might associate the "vanity of glory" with the image of Achilles, who in the underworld owns to Odysseus that he would rather be the last of slaves than a king over the dead; and we too, if we wish to illustrate that idea by an image, might think of a great ruler who by a contemplative life in his last years or by posthumous insight, had become aware of the nothingness of glory. Dante treats the matter differently. In the *Comedy* it is not Caesar who speaks of the emptiness of earthly glory; for Dante, Caesar's glory was not vain, but significant in the context of providential history. Actually, Dante required historical or mythical figures only when dealing with the great situations of political or religious history; for the concrete illustration of a mere ethical or empirical theme he had no need of them. And whom does he take as an example by which to illustrate the "vanity of glory?" The illuminator Oderisi of Gubbio, a contemporary (d. 1299) concerning whom nothing has come down to us but a note by Vasari, who even then knew very little about him. But even supposing him to have been the foremost in his art in Dante's time, what minuscule glory by which to illustrate so grandiose a theme! How many of Dante's contemporaries must have been ignorant of his very existence!—and yet Dante was confident that he would have readers in future centuries and wrote for them. But he required no brilliant example who would strike the reader by the contrast between his present state and the position, known to all, which he once occupied on earth; for him it was enough that Oderisi was known in his field and attached importance to his fame. The scene takes place among the proud, in the eleventh canto of the *Purgatorio;* as they move along ever so slowly, bowed almost to the ground beneath their heavy burdens, Dante speaks with one of them:

> *Ascoltando chinai in giù la faccia;*
> *Ed un di lor, non questi che parlava,*
> *Si torse sotto il peso che l'impaccia,*

> *E videmi e conobbemi e chiamava,*
> *Tenendo li occhi con fatica fisi*
> *A me che tutto chin con loro andava.*
> *"O!" diss'io lui: "Non se' tu Oderisi,*
> *L'onor d'Agobbio e l'onor di quell' arte*
> *Che 'alluminare' chiamata è in Parisi?"*
> *"Frate," diss' elli, "più ridon le carte*
> *Che pennelleggia Franco bolognese:*
> *L'onor è tutto or suo, e mio in parte.*
> *Ben non sare'io stato si cortese,*
> *Mentre ch'io vissi, per lo gran disio*
> *De l'eccellenza ove mio core intese.*
> *Di tal superbia qui si paga il fio. . . ."*

Listening I bent down my face; and one of them, not he
who was speaking, twisted himself beneath the weight
which encumbers him;

and saw me and knew me and was calling out keeping
his eyes with difficulty fixed upon me, who all bent
was going with them.

"Oh," said I to him, "are you not Oderisi, the honor of
Gubbio, and the honor of that art which in Paris is
called 'illuminating'?"

"Brother," said he, "more pleasing are the leaves which
Franco Bolognese paints; the honor now is all his and
mine in part.

Truly I should not have been so courteous while I lived,
because of the great desire of excellence on which my
heart was bent.

For such pride here the fine is paid. . . ."

After the poignant picture of recognition (*e videmi e conob-
bemi e chiamava*) Dante greets him with words of praise, for he
knows the other's weakness; but there is a faint note of conde-
scension and irony in Dante's words; ah, Gubbio's pride! One
also seems to discern the shadow of a smile in Dante's pointedly
circumspect way of referring to Oderisi's art. But how moving is
the penitent's answer! "Brother," says he, "more pleasing are the
leaves which Franco Bolognese paints. . . ." He is still preoccupied

with the rival, whose superiority, though he never acknowledged it, tormented him in his lifetime, and a part of his penance consists in acknowledging it now; these are the first words he utters, and then begins the well-known speech about fame, in which Cimabue and Giotto and the poets of the *stil nuovo* are mentioned. Here, then, a grandiose theme is illustrated by a man of small scope, whose immoderate lust for glory is grounded not in any great designs for domination and power but in the narrowness of his vision, whose "desire of excellence" was limited to a mere handicraft, though a beautiful one; the man was widely known, it is true, but his personality had not yet crystallized in the consciousnes of the public, and it was Dante who first fashioned a complete image of him as an ideal and typical representative of a vice and of the atonement by which this same vice is transcended. In that sense Dante is almost always the creator and first shaper of his figures. Cacciaguida declares, to be sure, that only souls known to fame, *che son di fama note,*[14] are presented to Dante in the Other World, because men would lend no credence to unknown examples. That may have been true for contemporary readers; yet even though Dante's contemporaries knew more than we do about the persons treated and though certain opinions about these figures may have been relatively widespread, it was Dante who, by identifying the reality of these men with their ultimate fate, first gave the opinions concerning them form and permanence. And for us, to whom very many of the dramatis personae are unknown, or who at best may have gleaned a fact or two about them from some historical document, Cacciaguida's words are no longer in any sense applicable; for us most of Dante's examples are no longer famous. And yet we do believe in them. One need only think of Francesca Malatesta da Rimini. In Dante's day her story may have been well known, today it is quite forgotten and nothing remains of it but the second half of the fifth canto of Dante's *Inferno*. But these lines have made her into a high poetic figure of historical, almost mythical stature.

Yet intermingled with the forgotten contemporaries of Dante, we also find the great figures of history and legend. Heroes and kings, saints and popes, princes, statesmen, generals, whose profiles even then had long been clearly engraved in the collective mind, appear in the place of their ultimate destiny and reveal their being. Dante always adheres to the tradition concerning them; but even there, as Gundolf[15] has clearly shown in connection with his Caesar, Dante is the creator of the figure. Just as in dealing with the persons he himself had known or of whom he had heard by word of mouth, he conjured up the sum of their gesture and fate from the contingent particulars of their lives, so here he distilled a real and evident figure from the records—so poor in sensuous images—of the medieval historians. He did not in every case establish them in the European mind: his image was often corrected at a later day through more accurate knowledge of the ancient spirit, though that too was first made possible by Dante. Dante's Homer with sword in hand[16] has been replaced by the Naples bust. But he was the first modern writer to lend them form: even though the ancient characters of the *Comedy* have been changed in passing through the medium of medieval reinterpretation, even though they have been transposed into a world order that is not always appropriate to their actuality, nevertheless, with Dante for the first time, that ordering, reinterpreting spirit of the Middle Ages provides something more than systematic edification. With Dante a new and imponderable element—compounded of poetry, experience, and vision—was gained for all time: but that should not make us forget that the force which guided him in his achievement sprang directly from the universalism of the rational doctrine he was striving to demonstrate by embodying it in a divine vision. The question: how does God see the earthly world?—and its answer: with all its particularities ordered with a view to the eternal goal—are the foundation of this profoundly passionate poem, and in its fifteen thousand lines there is not a scene or a magical chord which did not draw life from that rational foundation. Caesar stands before us unforgettable with his Suetonian *occhi grifagni* (his piercing eyes); Odysseus comes palpably to life; and Cato, however strangely interpreted, is a figure full of reality. But in each case what their eternal attitude shows is the concordance of their crucial traits with the providential course of the world, in which they acted thus and so and not otherwise; for all their radiant beauty they embody a rigorous doctrine. What a figure is Dante's

Odysseus![17] He is one of the few whose memory does not begin directly with the act that sealed his fate, the betrayal of Troy, mother of Rome; Dante may not address him, for the Greek would not reply; it is Virgil, the ancient poet who had sung of Greek heroes, who beseeches him to relate the end of his life. And cloaked in flames, Odysseus relates his last journey; how he found no peace at home, how his desire for knowledge and adventure drove him forth once more; how finally, old and tired, having already pressed forward as far as the Pillars of Hercules, he once again summons his companions to a bold undertaking:

> *"O frati," dissi "che per cento milia*
> *Perigli siete giunti a l'occidente*
> *A questa tanto picciola vigilia*
> *De'nostri sensi, ch'è del rimanente,*
> *Non vogliate negar l'esperienza,*
> *Diretro al sol, del mondo senza gente!*
> *Considerate la vostra semenza:*
> *Fatti non foste a viver come bruti*
> *Ma per seguir virtute e conoscenza."*

> "O brothers!" I said, "who through a hundred thousand
>   dangers have reached the West, deny not, to this brief
>   vigil
> of your senses that remains, experience of the unpeopled
>   world behind the Sun.
> Consider your origin; you were not formed to live like
>   brutes, but to follow virtue and knowledge."

In this narrative, which like a dream that interprets reality, discloses the unity of the European character in the spirit of world conquest that has carried down from Greek to modern times, one might be tempted to find an autonomous invention of character in the modern manner. It is only at the end of the story that its true meaning is laid bare. For five months Odysseus and his companions sail over the ocean; then they see a great mountain, but their joy is brief; the mountain is the Mountain of Purgatory, a cyclone rises up from it and the ship is wrecked. The providential order of the world has set a goal to human immoderation; the

boldness of Odysseus has no validity of its own; the human character finds its measure not in itself but in a destiny which is a
righteous judge. Yet despite that doctrine—and this, as we have
said, is characteristic of Dante's portraits of men—he is able to
preserve the autonomy of the character, and indeed Odysseus
even seems to gain in concrete presence from such rigorous eval-
uation and interpretation. Down to the most extreme particularity of his former sensuous being, the individual man is preserved
in the place of his ultimate fate: he is preserved in his physical
as well as his spiritual being. Physical and spiritual—the disjunction may give rise to a misunderstanding: what has been preserved is not two different things, but the unity of a single personality.

Dante saw many men, his vision was clear and precise; he was
no mere observer. And events that he did not see but only heard
or read of, sometimes in the most abstruse terms, became living
images for him: he heard the tone of his speakers, saw their
movements, sensed their hidden impulses, and thought their
thoughts. All these are one; and it is from that unity that he derives the figure. The gestures, the *manifestazioni plastiche,* the
plastic manifestations, as an Italian scholar[18] calls them, are never
an idle display of naturalistic observation; they have their ground
and limits in the event being narrated, and though at the same
time they manifest the person's physical being, such a concordance must follow inevitably from the concordance between the
personality and the event. We are given no details as to the appearance of Dante or Virgil; none of their physical traits is described and the one passage where something of the sort is said—
Beatrice's *"alza la barba"*[19] ("lift up your beard")—is very startling. But it is purely metaphorical, for it is quite certain that
Dante never wore a beard. However, a picture of them pieces itself together from the many scenes in which they speak and move
as the situation demands. And every single figure in the poem—
the glutton Ciacco, rising up in the murky rain and sinking back
again with revulsed eyes; Argenti biting himself; Casella coming
to meet Dante with open arms; the slothful Belacqua who sits
hugging his knees and barely raises his head at the unexpected
sight of a mortal—all show that naturalistic observation is gov-

erned and limited by the very definite event that is being related and that if the man nevertheless stands there complete, in all his sensuous fullness, it can only be because he is fully encompassed in the event. The gestures are few, but Dante tends to describe them with elaborate precision; he does not suggest, but describes or analyzes the actual movement, and often even that does not satisfy him: he tries to make it still clearer, and to accentuate it, by a long spun-out metaphor, which compels the reader to linger. When at the beginning of the poem he turns round to look back at the wooded valley, he unfolds the image of the swimmer who "has escaped from the deep sea to the shore," and still panting looks back over the perilous waters; at the end of the *Paradiso* he likens his immersion in the vision of God to a mathematician's increasing concentration on an insoluble problem. Between those two images lie the hundred cantos with their infinite wealth of metaphors, designed more often to clarify a concrete situation than a feeling. Perhaps more clearly than any other element of the work, they show the range and intensity of Dante's perception; animals and men, destinies and myths, idylls, warlike actions, landscapes, naturalistic street scenes, the most common periodic occurrence connected with the seasons and with men's occupations, the most personal recollection—everything is there: croaking frogs in the evening, a lizard darting across the path, sheep crowding out of their enclosure, a wasp withdrawing its sting, a dog scratching; fishes, falcons, doves, storks; a cyclone snapping off trees at the trunk; a morning countryside in spring, covered with hoarfrost; night falling on the first day of an ocean voyage; a monk receiving the confession of a murderer; a mother saving a child from fire; a lone knight galloping forth; a bewildered peasant in Rome; sometimes very brief, half a line— *attento si fermò com'uom che ascolta* (he stopped attentive like a man who listens)—sometimes rolling on at length, so that a landscape, an incident, a legend unfolds in all its breadth, always in order to serve the movement of the poem. This metaphoric technique, as we know, is ancient; some of the figures have even been taken from Virgil and many preserve something of the Virgilian tone; but the spirit and purpose are different. Virgil's metaphors are ornamental; they support the development only in the most general way, by evoking a similar, parallel idea; if they were removed, the poetic flow would be disturbed and the harmony of the picture would be impoverished, but the reality of the happening—which in any case is a vague, fairy-tale reality—would not be impaired. And Dante is still farther removed from his contemporaries who, like Guinizelli for example in his *Voglio del ver la mia donna laudare,* let their imagination roam, gathering up random scraps of all that is charming and resplendent, so losing their hold on the definite particular. Dante's metaphors are not parallel but concordant; they are intended not to ornament but to make clear; taken from the concrete, they lead to the concrete. That is why they are so much richer than those of Virgil and capable of performing a function that is more than lyrical; they are not only beautiful inventions—they serve to make reality more real; they help Dante to achieve the aim for which he invokes the help of the Muses: *sì che dal fatto il dir non sia diverso*[20] (so that my words may not be diverse from the fact).

What is said here of the metaphors is equally true of another poetic form which Dante took from his ancient models: the metamorphoses. In the *Comedy* the body is preserved along with the spirit; but the self-realization achieved in the hereafter brings about outward changes which sometimes destroy the former sensuous aspect completely. The change applies only to the appearance, not to the personality; on the contrary, the new appearance is a continuation, intensification, and interpretation of the old one and thus first discloses the real individual. In Dante, accordingly, metamorphosis loses its ancient fabulous character; from the remote darkness of legend it enters into present reality, for in every living man a metamorphosis may lie hidden: what man can say that he might not become a suicide? This apparent change is most drastic among the suicides and thieves: the suicides have become bushes[21] devoured and soiled by the Harpies; and the thieves undergo a strange transformation before Dante's eyes: set afire by snakebite, they either rise from their ashes or exchange aspects with a serpent.[22] Well-known figures of Dante's time incur those transformations, which embody a judgment on their former life; that is why the metamorphosis ceases to be mythical and enters the sphere of reality; the person who laments or scoffs or hisses or spits in that metamorphosed body is a very definite man whom many of Dante's contemporaries had known and whom all could imagine as one of their fellow men. Because Dante's metamorphosis is an individual human destiny, it is far more concrete than in Ovid or Lucan; the meeting with Pier della Vigna or the episode of the two Florentine thieves who exchange shapes, are set forth with an intensity and precision, they convey a degree of reality which is without parallel in ancient literature, precisely because, just as with the metaphors, the remote beauty of poetic illusion has been replaced by concrete truth taken as judgment.

In Paradise all the souls have undergone a transformation which human eyes cannot penetrate; they are hidden by the radiance of their beatitude and Dante cannot recognize them; they themselves must say who they are, and they cannot express their emotions by human gestures; strictly speaking, personal emotion can only manifest itself here by an increase in radiance. The danger of depersonalization and monotonous repetition is evident, and many believe that Dante succumbed to it and that the *Paradiso* lacks the poetic power of the first two parts of the *Comedy*. But such a criticism of Dante's *ultimo lavoro* springs from the Romantic prejudice of which we have spoken above[23] and shows that the critic has been unable to give himself to Dante's subject as a whole. The great similarity between the luminous manifestations, resulting from their common beatitude, does not exclude a preservation of the individual personality; the man is almost if not entirely hidden from the eyes, but he is there and finds means of making himself known. The disclosure is more tenuous and unmediated than in the other two parts; but it, too, has its root in the unique concordance between earthly life and ultimate fate, and the occasion for it, here again, is the meeting with the living Dante. Although the bodies are hidden, the luminous apparitions of the *Paradiso* have expressive gestures which accompany their memories of the former lives on earth; these are the different modes and movement of light, which Dante illustrates with an abundance of metaphors; the feminine souls of the moon appear as pearls on a white forehead; the souls of the sphere of Mercury gather round Dante like fish in clear water, swimming toward food that has been cast to them; an interruption of the dance when a new melody begins, the bells of the clock calling to Matins, the double circle of the rainbow: all interpret the phases of the dance in the sphere of the sun; as a shooting star falls to earth, so Cacciaguida's light descends from the cross of Mars upon his grandson, and the Triumph of Christ gives occasion for the unfolding of the most beautiful of all moonlit landscapes: *quale ne' plenilunii sereni . . .*,[24] as in the calm full moons. . . . The readers who intone such passages in a dreamy chanting tone and the interpreters who do their best to strip them of all meaning or purpose and regard them as pure inspiration, mystical, anonymous, and unrelated to the physical or spiritual world, in short, the modern view of poetry as the *ens realissimum* of intuition, which neither can nor need be carried back to its sources—all that is far removed from the spirit of Dante; for it is the truth of the rational doctrine which creates the concrete image and lends it power, and one who (as most readers do) remembers the passage but forgets that it refers to the Triumph of Christ is like a child picking raisins out of a cake; he gets very little of the taste of the cake. Such readers dwell too much on the *pasture da pigliar occhi per aver la mente,*[25] the food to catch the eyes and so possess the mind; they forget or rather overlook the fact that what is essential is *aver la mente,* to possess the mind; the sensuous manifestation, however beautiful, serves to communicate a rational thought, and it is only by way of the thought that one can judge whether the enchantment of the senses is sleight-of-hand or whether it is legitimate.

The same may be said of Dante's landscapes and chronological indications; they do not serve merely to bewitch the senses, and the mythical or astrological references in his chronologies are not a mere show of learning. Mythical erudition and sensuous enchantment both serve to bring out the reality, and that tangible reality—of morning or evening, a time of day or a season—is a mode or manifestation of the divine order. Just because it is always encompassed in the divine order, nature is imbued with spirit; it is a *natura sympathetica,* at once comprehending the whole and shot through with the spiritual significance of the literal events that take place in it. And from that unity of action and setting even the most violent expression derives measure and justification; because a line such as this—*Urlar li fa la pioggia come cani*[26] (The rain makes them howl like dogs)—is embedded in that unity, or concordance, there is measure even in its gruesome expressiveness.

Throughout the Other World the empirical reality is preserved; it fills us with delight or horror, but never surfeits us as is so often the case with the reality of our own lives; and never is the individual image contingent, blind, and fragmentary, the picture set before us is always a whole. Ordered and transfigured by the divine vision, earthly appearance becomes the true, definitive reality which, by its essence and the place in which it is manifested, discloses the plenitude of the divine order, so presupposing and encompassing everything else contained in it. The *Comedy* is an eminently philosophical work, not so much because of the actual philosophical doctrines set forth in it as because the spirit of those doctrines compels Dante to write philosophically. The subject, the *status animarium post mortem,* the state of the souls after death, constrains the poet, who holds the Christian belief in an individual justice for each man, to give concrete form to the idea of the individual; everything that is contingent or even temporal in his outward manifestation must be set aside, and yet the man himself, in his former unity of spirit and body, must be preserved in order that he may suffer or enjoy divine justice. Temporal relationships are at an end, and yet the a priori form of the individual, the fruit as it were of all his earthly acts and sufferings, is preserved. Very much in the manner of philosophy, which abstracts pure ideas from phenomena, this poetic work draws from earthly appearances the true personality which is body and spirit in one; it creates what might be called an ideal sensuous presence or a spirit endowed with a body that is necessary, concordant, and essential. All appearances are given their place in the true order of the other world, and that is the source of the *Comedy*'s necessary reality, of the *vital nutrimento,* the vital nutriment,[27] which Dante promises his readers.

Dante hoped for the favor of those *che questo tempo chiameranno antico*[28] (who shall call this time ancient)—and his hope has been fulfilled. But it did not occur to him that his work would one day be admired, in large part, by people to whom the foundations of his faith and world view had become meaningless and alien. He could never have conceived of such a thing, for like all his contemporaries he was lacking in historical sense, he was incapable of reconstructing an epoch on the basis of its own realities and presuppositions, rather than interpreting it in terms of his own time. His relation to Virgil was not very different from our relation to himself, for the spiritual and cultural foundations on which Virgil's art had arisen had crumbled and become utterly foreign to him. But of that he was quite unaware; he remodelled Virgil as though Augustan Rome were separated from his own epoch only by the passage of time, as though certain events had taken place and a certain amount of knowledge had been amassed in the meantime, but not as though man's whole form of life and thought had changed. Virgil the ancestor speaks the language of his descendant and profoundly understands him, whereas it would seem to us—Anatole France expressed the idea with a learned though somewhat facile elegance[29]—that if anyone had spoken to Virgil of Dante, he would not have understood him in the least, much less appreciated him. We possess at least a relatively better understanding of past or foreign cultures and are able to adapt ourselves to them rather than to take the opposite course like Dante; we are able, for a limited period and without binding ourselves, to accept strange forms and presuppositions very much as one accepts the rules of a game, and we do so in the hope of acquiring the feel of strange countries and their institutions and of learning to enjoy their art. In connection with Dante and a few others, no such transposition is necessary; anyone who understands his language and is capable of sympathy with human destinies can take in large parts of his work directly; the poem itself imperceptibly provides the necessary minimum of historical understanding. But there is another question that is more difficult to answer: can a modern reader, even if he is supremely learned and endowed with the highest degree of historical empathy, penetrate to Dante if he is utterly unwilling to accept Dante's mode of thought? Of course the greatest creations of the human spirit are not tied inseparably to the particular forms of thought and faith from which they sprang; they change with every generation that admires them, showing to each generation a new face without losing their intrinsic character. But there is a limit to their power of transformation; where the form of admiration becomes too arbitrary, they refuse to go along. To put it very cautiously, it seems to me that with regard to the *Divine Comedy* such a limit has almost been attained when philosophical commentators begin to praise its so-called poetic beauties as a value in themselves and reject the system, the doctrine, and indeed the entire subject matter as irrelevancies which if anything call for a certain indulgence.

The subject and doctrine of the *Comedy* are not incidental; they are the roots of its poetic beauty. They are the driving force behind the rich radiance of its poetic metaphors and the magical music of its verses; they are the form of the poem's matter, it is they which animate and kindle the poet's sublime fantasy; it is they which lend the vision its true form and with it the power to move us and enchant us. Firm in that belief, we conclude this part of our investigation with Dante's apostrophe to Fantasy:

> *O imaginativa che non rube*
> *Talvolta si di fuor, ch'om non s'accorge*
> *Perchè dintorno suonin mille tube,*
> *Chi move te, se il senso non ti porge?*
> *Moveti lume che nel ciel s'informa*
> *Per sè o per voler che giù lo scorge.*[30]

> O fantasy, that at times so snatch us out of ourselves that we are conscious of nothing, even though a thousand trumpets sound about us,
> Who moves you, if the senses set nothing before you? A light moves you which takes its form in heaven, of itself, or by a will that sends it down.

The content of the *Comedy* is a vision; but what is beheld in the vision is the truth as concrete reality, and hence it is both real and rational. Consequently the language which communicates the truth is at once that of a record and of a didactic treatise. It is the language of a record, not of an epic: for the fantasy is not free to roam in a distant legendary land; rather, the speaker is a witness who has seen everything with his own eyes and is expected to give an accurate report: he has seen something more miraculous than any legend, and he does not say: "Muse, name to me the man . . . ," or "Once upon a time King Arthur held a royal feast at the Pentecost"; he begins: "In the middle of my life I found myself in a dark forest." The language is also that of a didactic treatise, for what is beheld in the vision is Being or truth; it is always rationally ordered, and until close before the threshold of the actual *visio Dei* it is accessible to disciplined rational discourse.

An almost severely accurate record of events and dogmatic instruction, rational to the point of pedantry—these are the determining factors in the style of the *Comedy*. They are never wholly distinguishable and as a rule they are thoroughly blended; there is no happening that does not illustrate the doctrine and no teaching that is not based on concrete happening. But fantasy, the essential element of poetry—and that applies equally to the epic fantasy which freely links, transforms, spins out events drawn from a remote legendary sphere, and to the lyrical fantasy which spurns rational limits in order to arouse and give free voice to that which knows no limits, to feeling—has lost its autonomy in the *Comedy*. The poem contains incomparable examples of both epic and lyrical fantasy, of richly diversified happening, and of deep feeling, eloquently expressed. But neither one is free or dominant. The event is recounted briefly and succinctly, seldom taking the form of a tale and never of a rambling legend; among others of its kind it always preserves its strictly appointed place and never ceases to be subordinate to a higher principle; and the strongest feeling is always described with precision, in just so much space, as though measured out; it is so wholly contained in the lines devoted to it, so quickly and definitively disposed of, that all lyrical resonance is cut off and it is impossible to linger on it.

It is the subordination of the richest fantasy to the didactic record that gives the language of the *Comedy* the concentrated power which is its most salient characteristic. The first demand that the revealed truth makes on one who sets out to communicate it, is accuracy. The revealed truth is exactly as it is, strictly circumscribed in its form and limits, and that is how it demands to be represented: the narrator must speak sharply and clearly; avoiding all lyrical rambling or rhetorical prolixity, he must always reproduce what he has seen or felt in its true, exact measures. An example comes to mind: the Provençal lament for the young King Henry of England begins with a very beautiful period, one of the finest to have been written before Dante:

> *Si tuit li dol e lh plor e lh marrimen*
> *E las dolors e lh dan e lh chaitivier*
> *Que om anc auzis en est segle dolen*
> *Fossen ensems, sembleran tot leugier*
> *Contra la mort del jove rei engles. . . .*[31]

If all the mourning and tears and sorrow, and the pain and the loss and the evil that have been seen in this doleful century, were massed together, they would seem as nothing beside the death of the young King of England. . . .

To the rhetorical vagueness produced by such accumulation (mourning, tears, sorrow, etc.) let us compare a line in which Dante measures out an overpowering grief: *Tant'e amara, che poco è più morte*[32] (So bitter is it that scarcely more is death). Terrible is the wood, how terrible it is hard to say; death is only a little more, yet it is more, and the rationality of that truth compels the poet to measure his experience exactly; it forbids him to fill in the picture with nonessentials, it subjugates his poetic resources and extends its power even to the alliteration between the broad lingering *amara* and the hard, biting *morte*. The sentence structure as well, with its comparative *tanto che,* which Dante employs so frequently, has nothing ornamental about it, but quite to the contrary conveys the precise measurement of a mathematical equation; and though other comparisons contained in the great poem may carry ever so much lyrical enchantment, their purpose is not ornament, they are equations of measure; sometimes, very rarely, a learned recollection or the exigencies of his *terza rima* may drive him beyond the necessary measure—I shall not quote any passage, for it is a question of feeling, and I can quite well imagine that to another reader the occasional passages that strike me as excessive may seem perfectly necessary and appropriate. Even then the end result is a definite, precise picture and never a lyrical or rhetorical approximation which moves the imagination without setting limits and satisfying the mind. It was that precision which led Dante himself and many of his critics to judge the style of the *Comedy* as half poetic and half prosaic. An example chosen at random, a sentence such as this: *E poi, così andando, mi disse: "Perchè sei tu sì smarrito?"*[33] (And then, as we were going, he said to me: "Why are you so bewildered?") seems quite prosaic and matter-of-fact when lifted out of its context; and from such sentences, from the fact that Dante did not hesitate to write them, it can be inferred that other, more poetic, more imaged, more indirect sentences—such as, *"perchè la tua faccia testeso un lampeggiar di riso dimostrommi?"*[34] ("Wherefore did your face but now display to me a flash of laughter?"), or *"Scocca l'arco del dir,"* etc.[35] ("Discharge the bow of your speech which you have drawn to the iron")—were not written for the sake of an autonomous image. No one who reads with open eyes the most brilliant passages in the *Comedy,* those known for their poetic power—the lines at the beginning of the *Inferno* or the prayer *Vergine madre*—can deny that they are full to the brim with precise dogmatic instruction transformed into concrete images: *"Vergine madre, figlia del tuo figlio, umile e alta più che creatura, termine fisso d'eterno consiglio, tu se' colei che l'umana natura nobilitasti sì, che il suo fattore non disdegnò di farsi sua fattura. Nel ventre tuo si raccese l'amore per lo cui caldo ne l'eterna pace così è germinato questo fiore."*[36] ("Virgin mother, daughter of your son, lowly and uplifted more than any creature, fixed goal of the eternal counsel, you are she who so ennobled human nature that its own maker scorned not to become its making. In your womb was lit again the love under whose warmth in the eternal peace this flower has thus unfolded.") This is doctrine, and though such a companion piece as the *Stabat mater* can hardly be suspected of immoderate lyricism, the lyrical and legendary elements in it have far greater autonomy; Thomas of Celano goes to much greater length in painting the lyrical aspects of the legend. And merely has use of a rhetorical turn such as:—*Quis est homo qui non fleret, Christi matrem si videret* (Who is the man who would not weep were he to see the mother of Christ), which would be quite inconceivable in Dante, shows the enormous difference between a purely lyrical effusion, even dealing with the fact of the Passion, and the record of the revealed truth presented in the *Comedy*. Dante too sometimes steps out of the poem. "Thou reader!" he cries, or "Ye of sound intellect!" But then he addresses himself directly to definite persons, to an opposite, almost as though a teacher were calling on a pupil, and he calls attention to a definite object. The precision with which Dante speaks even in the most lyrical passages—*per chiare parole e con preciso latin*[37] (in clear words and with precise discourse)—is equally evident in his choice of words, in his phonetic devices, his syntax, and his rhymes. Even in the poetry of his youth, we have praised his power of apprehending reality; but here that power is vastly enriched by the richer subject matter and the deeper experience, and at the same time more strictly circumscribed by the clear nature of the task. No word is too crass or too plain for him; he summons all the senses to help him, the most common, everyday experience has its place if it helps to give his thought concreteness; such figures as *tu proverai sì come sa di sale lo pane altrui*[38] (You shall make trial of how salty another's bread tastes) or as the likening of St. Bernard, who compares the white rose of heaven, to the good tailor who cuts a coat as the cloth permits,[39] and in general the material metaphors frequently employed to represent inner experience penetrate, with a hitherto unknown purposiveness and sureness of aim, to the very heart of his subject. And likewise his handling of sound is wholly attuned to his purpose. The phonetic repetition employed by Beatrice in speaking of Virgil's fame (*dura, durerà,* "endures" and "will endure"[40])—one example among many—, a landscape painted in sound and rhythm—*lo dì c'han detto ai dolci amici addio*[41] (the day when they have said goodbye to their sweet friends) or, in a different rhythm, *e cigola per vento che va via*[42] (and hisses with the escaping wind)—none of these figures dismisses the reader with a mere impression; he is compelled to take note of the concrete reality, to which Dante always subordinates his extraordinary technical resources.

Often the sentence structure is almost prosaic, as a rule it is designedly paratactic and simple: the period exactly coincides with a tercet, and pauses called for by the meaning exactly fall at the end of a line and the rhyme. Yet the sharpness of the connections, the precise use of conjunctions, by which the vast subject matter is really articulated and controlled, create a new language of thought. Dante has transformed and breathed new life into the classical period. It would take us too far to speak of the rhetorical prescriptions of the duecento, of the curial style, and of the artes dictandi; suffice it to note that the language of the *Summa theologica,* the greatest intellectual monument of the time, is by no means as rich as that of the *Comedy,* and scarcely more precise in its logic. Before Dante a thought such as the following, with all its complex articulations, could not possibly have been treated as a unit: *"Tu dici che di Silvio lo parente, corruttibile ancora, ad immortale secolo andò, e fu sensibilmente: però se l'avversario d'ogni male cortese i fu, pensando l'alto effetto che uscir dovea di lui, e il chi, e il quale, non pare indegno ad omo d'intelletto; ch'ei fu dell'alma Roma e di suo impero nell'empireo ciel per padre eletto; la quale e il quale, a voler dir lo vero, fur stabiliti per lo loco santo, u' siede il successor del maggior Piero. Per questa andata onde gli dai tu vanto, intese cose che furon cagione di sua vittoria e del papale ammanto; andovvi poi ... ma mio. ..."*[43] (You say that the father of Sylvius, while subject to corruption, went to the immortal world and was there in body. But if the adversary of all evil was propitious to him, considering the high effect, and who and what should come from him, it seems not unfitting to an understanding mind: for in the empyreal heaven, he was chosen to be the father of generous Rome, and of her Empire; but these, to say the truth, were established for the holy place, where the Successor of the greatest Peter sits. By this journey, for which you honour him, he learned things that were the cause of his victory, and of the Papal mantle. Afterwards ... But I. ....") And it is evident that this syntactic skill stems from the systematic concreteness of the vision which demands to be set forth with precision.

Yet in demanding precise expression the divine truth demands the impossible; for such expression of the divine far exceeds the poet's powers, and though grace enhances his gifts at certain decisive moments, he is unequal to the enormous task of describing his vision after his return to earth. In the opening lines of the second canto of the *Inferno,* the contrast with which he describes the awakening of fear at the thought of the great journey ahead of him leads him (as happens very rarely) to end the tercet with the opening words of the next sentence: *ed io sol uno* (and I, one alone); it is followed by a cry of supplication to the Muses and to his own powers—*o mente che scrivesti ciò ch'io vidi*[44] (O Memory, that has inscribed what I saw)—not to forsake him in his overpowering task. Though here and in some later passages he speaks with proud confidence of his own work, in Paradise he becomes increasingly aware of his human inadequacy: his mortal shoulders can scarcely bear the burden, and more than once the sacred poem must "make a leap as one who finds his pathway intercepted." The superhuman difficulty of the task is clearly discernible in the language of the poem; for although the *Comedy,* considered as a whole, seems astonishingly light and simple—thanks to its clear and orderly structure— there is no single passage that does not reflect tension and effort; one is left with the impression that the work at every step demanded of Dante a boundless devotion, an unstinting expenditure of himself. If the passage *Se mai continga*[45] (Should it e'er come to pass) required any commentary to heighten its effect, it might be the thought that the man grown lean who had written these lines felt his end approaching, felt that if he were to witness the event of which he is speaking, it must happen soon. Nearly every line of the *Comedy* reveals enormous exertion; the language writhes and rebels in the hard fetters of rhyme and meter; the form of certain lines and sentences suggests a man frozen or petrified in a peculiarly unnatural position: they are monumentally clear and expressive, but strange, terrifying, and superhuman. That is why Dante is associated with Michelangelo in the popular mind. Dante employs deviation from natural word order more frequently and radically than any other medieval stylist. Suddenly, without appeasing harmony, one of these periods takes its place by the side of a perfectly prosaic sentence, often made up of the most everyday words. He may have learned this device from Virgil and classical poetics, but Virgil did have appeasing harmony, and the classical languages had a tradition of poetic word order which made it possible to identify the device as such, to examine it and find it good or bad. Dante created his own tradition; when he broke up a sentence, isolating or transposing certain words, separating what belonged together or juxtaposing elements that are ordinarily separate, he was engaged in an instinctive striving for concordant expression, quite distinct from the aesthetic considerations that may have found a place in his earlier writings. Such artifices are employed with an instinctive directness, and it is with equal directness that they assail the reader, who in every single case must reflect for some time before he realizes exactly what manner of device has had this effect on him. Dante introduced these sudden breaks in word order into an almost prosaic narrative which not infrequently enumerates and circumscribes with a precision so elaborate as to give an effect of unevenness, and the combination is the source of the *Comedy*'s lofty tone, a tone attained by no other poet than Dante, which anyone who has once heard it will always remember and always identify with Dante. And yet this noble language, in which there is so much learning and tradition, is rooted so immediately in the subject matter and the striving to give it appropriate expression, and Dante displays such sovereignty in his treatment of traditional devices, here employing them, there spurning them, and then again transforming them into something utterly new, that we shall perhaps do best to say that with Dante a new, a second nature sprang from the soil of the traditional stylistic devices.

> *Ruppemi l'alto sonno nella testa*
> *Un greve tuono*[46]

A heavy thunder broke the deep sleep in my head.

So Dante describes a sudden awakening. When closely examined, this passage, with its almost painfully concrete image—sleep broken in his head—with its unaccustomed accentuation of the verb which starts the sentence while the subject comes at the end, seems to be carefully calculated for its effect, and perhaps it is. But our first feeling is that a direct inspiration is at work, and our first feeling is right, for Dante had at his command an inspiration which did not exclude the observing, measuring, calculating powers of the intellect, but enhanced them; and the consequence is that his memory of Virgilian style, his concern with what was to follow, with his rhyme and syllable count were able to operate undisturbed, neither overwhelmed by the hurricane of his feeling, nor breaking its power. For the singling out of a word, a device also employed by the Provençal poets, though with less sharpness, the line just cited is one among many:[47] sometimes the effect is sweet and emphatic as in *Biondo era e bello e di gentile aspetto*[48] (Golden-haired was he, and fair, and of noble mien), and sometimes harsh, pointing up a crass antithesis:

> *e cortesia fu lui esser villano*[49]
> and to be rude to him was courtesy

and in still other passages, this emphatic dislocation of a sentence seems to dissect an action, to show that it is slow and gradual, as in the stoning of St. Stephen:

> *e lui vedea chinarri per la morte,*
> *che l'aggravava già, inver la terra;*
> *ma degli occhi facea sempre al ciel porte*[50]
> And him I saw bowed to the earth by death,
> which weighed upon him now, but of his eyes he
> made ever gates to heaven.

But the listing of examples can easily be misleading, because we should have them all before us; in reference to any one a contradictor might say that the effect is accidental, springing primarily from the exigencies of rhyme or some other technical consideration, and only a great number of examples can force us to see how perpetual conflict compels the inner and outward forces to work together. Even so, I shall have to cite a few more examples. In considering the sentence: "Whoever you are turn around," how unpleasant it is to be constrained to account for the position of "Whoever" by the rhyme:

> *chiunque*
> *tu sei, così andando volgi il viso.*[51]

And yet the *chiunque,* also in sound and meaning, is so magnificent an anacrusis to the rhythm of what follows, that it is difficult to decide whether the motive was necessity or subtle purpose. The exigency of rhyme surely has something to do with the unequal structure of the two terms of the antithesis

> *Lunga promessa con l'attender corto*[52]
> Large promise with small observance of it

but who would not rejoice at such necessity? Dante's poetry is a constant struggle with the object and the form it demands, a contest of hard with hard, in which the poet is always victorious; but at the end of the struggle the defeated object is new-born and young in the form the poet has given it, while the victor is exhausted and ready to die. The unusual varieties of sentence structure are by no means the only signs of the struggle: we must try to feel what effort went into this heaping up of antitheses round the same word:

> *Amor, ch'a null'amato amar perdona*[53]
> Love, which to no loved one permits excuse for loving

or

> *Ma vince lei perche vuol esser vinta*
> *e vinta vince con sua beninanza*[54]
>
> but conquers it because it wills to be conquered,
> and conquered, with its own benignity doth conquer.

We must try to understand a poet who, not content to compare the brevity of a moment of Creation with a ray of light, makes the ray of light fall upon a transparent substance, glass, amber, or crystal

> *sì che dal venire*
> *Al esser tutto non è intervallo,*[55]
>
> so that from its coming to its pervading all, there is
> no interval.

What an exhausting immersion in reality there is in such an image! It is Dante's own struggle that creates the noble tone in his poem. With powers scarcely his own, powers instilled in him by his task, which continue to grow, and he with them, and will depart from him when the poem is finished—he hews words out of himself, as though from his own flesh, and to each single one he gives new roots and new life in its appointed place. Is there any other poem, particularly one of such length, in which each single word, taken by itself, seems so autonomous a creation, so much a living, organic, and clearly delimited reality? Dante puts his words in place as though forming them anew, as though an architect were to take his stone direct from the quarry, to hew and shape the masonry himself. And he could not have done otherwise: his subject, a perfect transcendent world, demanded a fresh creation with suitable materials; it gave Dante the highest expressive power and consumed his strength. The strain on his powers increases as the poem advances; and behind the startlingly sudden turnabout at the end, behind the last line with its double caesura, with its flow of feeling abruptly broken off and haltingly resumed, an image has risen time and time again in my mind: the poet sinking back in exhaustion.

Because the configured truth is exact and superhuman, it demands precision and superhuman powers of its poet; and similarly, it demands order of him because it is ordered. The sacred number three is reflected in the three parts of the poem, in the number of cantos, in the tercets, and in the *terza rima;* and a language must be devised that will frame this interlocking order in tercets. As we have said, the constraint does not hamper the poet's many-sided freedom, but creates and furthers freedom; what is born of such constraint is not artifice or mannerism, but a second nature, hard come by but all the richer for that. The natural formal unity of the poem is achieved by the interlocking of the two threefold orders; the anticipating rhyme of the middle line, to which the following tercet responds, binds the cantos into unbroken chains, in which every link, though itself a perfectly independent three, is inseparably forged together with the preceding and the following three. And the rigidity, one may even say monotony, of the metric structure, the inexorable recurrence of the rhyme, always at the same place in the rhythmic pattern, does not detract from the variety of movement; the distribution of rhythmic pauses, the rise and fall of the tone, the possibility of singling out words or letting them flow together—all that is preserved; the movement is so variegated and free that the rhythmic surge of the *Comedy,* despite the dikes that hem it in, has been justly likened to the ocean; and like the ocean, it discloses every shading from storm to perfect calm. Here again it is undeniable that the resistance of the ordering principle strengthens the inner movement of the language; it gives the rhythmic figures the self-sufficiency, the monumental solidity that a freer form could not have attained. For where the form is more varied, every movement is filled with the present, and for its sake what has gone before is forgotten; but here every part, however self-contained, stands for the whole, calls the whole to mind, mirrors it in an eminently Thomist sense, without in the least losing its own character. Thus in the *Comedy* no particular of rhythmic expression is lost; every rhythm is in itself a living thing, impelled by the narrowness of the space within which it must move to live all the more intensely and self-sufficiently, and every rhythm is contained and mirrored in each of the innumerable variations that follow; wherever you may open the *Comedy,* you have the whole of it. Furthermore, the strictness of his metric structure, in which meaning and rhythm are almost merged as it were, has enabled Dante to employ a stylistic device which is tremendously effective just because it is unusual and seemingly at variance with the prevailing law; in moments of extreme feeling, the surge overflows the dike of the rhyme that concludes the line. At the beginning of his pilgrimage, after telling of the nightfall that frees the creatures of the earth from the toils of the day, Dante is led by his awareness of the impending struggle to leave the tercet hanging in midair; from the evening landscape the *ed io sol uno m'apparecchiava*[56] (and I, one alone, was preparing) rises like a sudden storm, flinging itself into the next line without regard for the pause normally expected at the end of a tercet. There are not many examples of this; nor may we automatically omit the pause wherever a sentence oversteps the end of a line; on the contrary, where doubt is possible the end of a line does signify a pause. But a few passages are perfectly plain. In the tercet speaking of Buonconte's death—

> *Quivi perdei la vista, e la parola*
> *nel nome di Maria finii; e quivi*
> *caddi....*[57]

There lost I vision, and ended my words upon the name
of Mary; and there I fell . . .

a brief pause seems possible after *parola;*[58] but *e quivi* and *caddi* belong together.

Finally, we must mention a fourth aspect of the configured truth: it demands acceptance; the poem that contains it must be compelling. The authority of the witness who with his own eyes has seen what is most important in a man, namely his true person and his ultimate fate, must be so strong that the reader cannot doubt or be left indifferent, but is convinced and carried away. In the second chapter we have spoken of how the youthful Dante, by the summons and conjuration of his apostrophes, was able to choose his listeners and to hold them spellbound within a magic circle: the language of the *Divine Comedy* also has the character of conjuration, not only where the poet speaks directly to the reader, but from the very beginning and throughout. The rigorous directness with which Dante immediately sets forth the extreme peril of the situation, the depths of his distress and the one hope of salvation, gives the record of his journey the value of personal testimony. In the *Comedy* all the characters are interpreted, their individual destinies have been fulfilled; only Dante himself, the wanderer, is in a state of uncertainty, still unfulfilled and subject to interpretation. In the uncertainty of his wandering in the forest, in the Other World which he explores and where he alone has as yet no definite place, he is living man in general, and every other living man can identify himself with him. The human drama, the danger confronting all who live—these are the framework of the vision; his perplexity and Virgil's mission, the three bestowers of grace, the liberation at the summit of Purgatory, the meeting with Beatrice, and the ascent to the vision of God—these are the great stations in the drama of Dante; his vision of the Other World is only an experience of the living man's imperilled soul, and the witness becomes a hero. In relation to his hearers Dante is a messenger bearing not only the most important of messages, but a message concerning himself. The pilgrim to the realms of the Other World has embarked on his journey because it is his only possible road to salvation: this is what gives his report its compelling earnestness and what gives his emotions the universal power that carries over to the reader. The torment and delight of his own experience—*la guerra sì del cammino, e sì della pietate*[59] (the war both of the journey and the pity) mold his language; he has not been sent by others to learn, it is for himself that he learns, and with all his being he clings to what is shown him; everything that he sees befalls him personally. In any scene we may choose, in the episodes of Francesca or Farinata, of Casella or Forese, Charles Martell or Cacciaguida, we can observe how his spirit comes, in fear and yearning, to each encounter; his emotions are described with all his characteristic power of embodiment. Who, for example, can dispel the pressure of dread on reading such a line as *ed io ch'avea d'orror la testa cinta*[60] (And I my head begirt with horror)?

These elements—reality and superhuman will, order and compelling authority—are the substance of the *Comedy*'s style, which is so unique that anyone who knows the work well has the impression of hearing Dante's voice in every word and every tone: a powerful voice, sternly admonishing, yet full of tenderness, a voice which for all its severity is always human. In uttering what is true and right, it takes the tone of a teacher; in recording real events it becomes a chronicler. But doctrine and chronicle are caught up in the poetic movement, sustained and exalted until, with all their clarity, they stand before us unapproachable and inexplicably perfect. The *Comedy,* as we have repeatedly said in the course of this investigation, treats of earthly reality in its true and definitive form; but palpable and concrete as this reality is, it takes on an ethereal dreamlike quality in the Other World. As we have seen, the later Provençal poets, the poets of the *stil nuovo,* and Dante himself in the poetry of his youth, had followed an old esoteric tradition in setting apart the noble devotees of *Amore* from the rest of mankind and in regarding them alone as a worthy audience. That tradition like many others is transformed but not abandoned in the *Comedy*. Here I am not referring to the occasional apostrophes to one another of the chosen few; they are not crucial in this connection, for there is no doubt that the *Comedy* as a whole is addressed to all men or at least to all Christians. What I have in mind is that he leads *all* men into a realm apart, where the air is not that of our everyday earth. Not that the reality of life has vanished; it has grown doubly plain and tangible. But the light is different and the eyes must grow accustomed to it; they must acquire a new and sharper vision which passes over no detail as unimportant, commonplace, or fragmentary; whatever appears in that place is definitive and immutable, demanding the fullest and most careful attention. Dante transports his listeners into a strange world so permeated by the memory of reality that it seems real while life itself becomes a fragmentary dream; and that unity of reality and remoteness is the source of his psychological power.

VI

THE SURVIVAL AND TRANSFORMATION OF
DANTE'S VISION OF REALITY

Here we shall not speak in the usual sense of Dante's influence on posterity. Neither the few insignificant poets who have imitated the *Comedy,* nor the highly problematic influence of Dante's ideas and teachings, nor the far more important "history of his fame"—in short, no part of what is known in Italy as *la fortuna di Dante*—can have any bearing on the present study. Here we are concerned with something he created and which remained living and effective, quite regardless of whether those in whom we find it followed his doctrines or not, of whether they loved or hated him, or, for that matter, of whether they were even familiar with his work. For the land he discovered has not been lost; many have entered upon it, some have explored it, though the fact that he was first to discover it has been largely forgotten or ignored. The something of which I am speaking, the discovery that remained alive, is Dante's testimony to the reality that is poetry, to the modern European form of artistic mimesis which stresses the actuality of events.

Stefan George[1] speaks of tone, movement, and Gestalt—it is they, he says, that make Dante the father of all modern literature. And perhaps not only of literature. Dante discovered the European representation (Gestalt) of man, and this same representation made its appearance in art and historiography. Dante was the first to configure what classical antiquity had configured very differently and the Middle Ages not at all: man, not as a remote legendary hero, not as an abstract or anecdotal representative of an ethical type, but man as we know him in his living historical reality, the concrete individual in his unity and wholeness; and in that he has been followed by all subsequent portrayers of man, regardless of whether they treated a historical or a mythical or a religious subject, for after Dante myth and legend also became history. Even in portraying saints, writers have striven for truth to life, for historical concreteness, as though saints too were a part of the historical process. As we have seen, Christian legend came to be treated as an immanent historical reality; the arts have striven to represent a more perfect unity of spirit and body, spun into the fabric of man's destiny, and despite changes of taste and differences in artistic technique, this striving has endured, through many perils and darkenings, down to our day.

In the present work, we have tried to show that this immense conquest did not spring full-blown from Dante's intuition, but that his creative powers were kindled by his subject, which compelled him, once he had undertaken to set forth the divine judgment, to unearth the complete truth about individual historical men, and consequently to reveal the whole character and personality. As we have repeatedly stressed, his poetic genius was inseparably bound up with his doctrine. But his doctrine did not endure. The *Comedy* represented the physical, ethical, and political unity of the Scholastic Christian cosmos at a time when it was beginning to lose its ideological integrity: Dante took the attitude of a conservative defender, his battle was an attempt to regain something that had already been lost; in this battle he was defeated, and his hopes and prophecies were never fulfilled. True, ideas of a Roman World Empire survived down to the Late Renaissance, and indignation over the corruption of the Church led to the great movements of the Reformation and Counter Reformation. But those ideas and movements have only certain superficial characteristics in common with Dante's view of the world; they originated and grew independently of it. Some were fantastic dreams, some were great popular uprisings, some acts of practical politics, and still others had something of all three: but none possessed the depth and universal unity of

Dante's Thomist world view, and their consequence was not the worldwide *humana civilitas* for which Dante hoped, but an increasing fragmentation of cultural forces; it is only after the imperial ideology and the Christian-medieval conception of the world, shaken by intestine struggles, were swept away by the rationalism of the seventeenth and eighteenth centuries that a new practical view of the unity of human society began to take form. Thus Dante's work remained almost without influence on the history of European thought; immediately after his death, and even during his lifetime, the structure of literary, cultured society underwent a complete change in which he had no part, the change from Scholastic to Humanistic thinking, and that transformation undermined the influence of so rigorously committed a work as the *Comedy*. The radical shift in values that has taken place is made clear by the example of Petrarch, who was only forty years younger than Dante. Petrarch was not actually of a different party, he was not opposed to Dante's strivings; but what moved Dante, the whole attitude and form of his life, had grown alien to him. He is distinguished from Dante above all by his new attitude toward his own person; it was no longer in looking upward—as Orcagna portrayed Dante in his fresco of the Last Judgment in Santa Maria Novella—that Petrarch expected to find self-fulfillment, but in the conscious cultivation of his own nature. Although far inferior to Dante in personality and natural endowment, he was unwilling to acknowledge any superior order or authority; not even the authority of the universal world order to which Dante submitted so passionately. The autonomous personality, of which Petrarch was to be the first fully typical modern European embodiment, has lived in a thousand forms and varieties; the conception takes in all the tendencies of the modern age, the business spirit, the religious subjectivism, the humanism, and the striving for physical and technological domination of the world. It is incomparably richer, deeper, and more dangerous than the ancient cult of the person. From Christianity, whence it rose and which it ultimately defeated, this conception inherited unrest and immoderation. These qualities led it to discard the structure and limits of Dante's world, to which, however, it owed the power of its actuality.

Accordingly, even if it is agreed that Dante's creation is closely bound up with his subject matter, that his poetry is inseparable from his doctrine, he seems to be a special case that has never been repeated and hence tells us nothing about the nature of the poetic process. For the art of imitating reality continued to develop quite independently of the presuppositions which seem to have been at the base of Dante's work. No poet or artist after Dante required an ultimate, eschatological destiny in order to perceive the unity of the human person: sheer intuitive power seems to have enabled subsequent writers to combine inner and outward observation into a whole.

But that argument does not take in the whole truth. Its proponents neglect or underestimate the part played in the creative drive by the residues of older intellectual forces and fail to discern such residues beneath superficial changes in consciousness. It is generally acknowledged that the Renaissance represents a unit in the history of European culture and that the decisive element of its unity was the self-discovery of the human personality; and it is also generally recognized that, despite Dante's medieval view of the world, the discovery began with him. Thus there would seem to be reason to believe that something in the structure of the medieval world view was carried over into the new development and made it possible. In the history of modern European culture, there is, indeed, a constant which has come down unchanged through all the metamorphoses of religious and philosophical forms, and which is first discernible in Dante; namely, the idea (whatever its basis may be) that individual destiny is not meaningless, but is necessarily tragic and significant, and that the whole world context is revealed in it. That conception was already present in ancient mimesis, but carried less force, because the eschatological myths of the ancients lent far less support than Christian doctrine and the story of Christ to the conviction that the individual is indestructible, that the life of the individual on earth is a brief moment of irrevocable decision. In the early Middle Ages the historical sense had been dulled—the image of man was reduced to a moral or spiritualist abstraction, a remote legendary dream, or a comic caricature; in short man was removed from his natural, historical habitat. With Dante the historical individual was reborn in his manifest unity of body and spirit; he was both old and new, rising from long oblivion with greater power and scope than ever before. And although the Christian eschatology that had given birth to this new vision of man was to lose its unity and vitality, the European mind was so permeated with the idea of human destiny that even in very un-Christian artists it preserved the Christian force and tension which were Dante's gift to posterity. Modern mimesis found man in his individual destiny; it raised him out of the two-dimensional unreality of a remote dreamland or philosophical abstraction, and moved him into the historical area in which he really lives. But that historical world had to be rediscovered; and in a spiritualist culture, where earthly happening was either disregarded or looked upon as a mere metaphorical existence leading up to man's real and final destiny, man's historical world could be discovered only by way of his final destiny, considered as the goal and meaning of earthly happening. But once the discovery was made in that way, earthly happening could no longer be looked upon with indifference. The perception of history and immanent reality arrived at in the *Comedy* through an eschato-logical vision, flowed back into real history, filling it with the blood of authentic truth, for an awareness had been born that a man's concrete earthly life is encompaseed in his ultimate fate and that the event in its authentic, concrete, complete uniqueness is important for the part it plays in God's judgment. From that center man's earthly, historical reality derived new life and value, and even the *Comedy* where, not without difficulty, the turbulent new forces were confined within an eschatological frame, gives us an intimation of how quickly and violently they would break loose. With Petrarch and Boccaccio the historical world acquired a fully immanent autonomy, and this sense of the self-sufficiency of earthly life spread like a fructifying stream to the rest of Europe—seemingly quite estranged from its eschatological origin and yet secretly linked with it through man's irrevocable bond with his concrete historical fate.

By that I do not mean that literature and art began to concern themselves exclusively with subjects drawn from real life and history, and no such statement would be in keeping with the facts. Mythical and religious subjects continued to be treated, and indeed more penetratingly than before. For they too were drawn into the historical vision we have described; the traditional fable lost its emblematic rigidity, and from the rich material, which had been largely obscured beneath dogmatic and spiritualist symbols, the author was now enabled, by his insight into the unity of character and fate, to select the perceptions that seemed to offer the fullest evidence and the most essential truth. And another form of literature, which is perhaps the most significant of all in modern Europe because it has permeated all others, namely the lyrical self-portraiture initiated by Petrarch, was rendered possible only by the discovery of the historical world. For it was only in that area that the diverse levels of feeling and instinct, the entire unity and variety of the personality, could unfold, that the empirical person, the individual with his inner life, could become an object of mimesis.

This current created rich new possibilities and grave dangers for mimesis. To discuss them is not the purpose of the present book, in which I have tried to grasp Dante's work as a unity, rooted in the unity of his subject matter. It has seemed to me that this approach offered the only hope of representing Dante's historical reality in such a way that "the words may not be diverse from the fact."

NOTES

The following is a list of abbreviations of the books most frequently cited in the notes. All references to Dante's works are to the edition given below.

Ed. Anglade   Anglade, Joseph (ed.). *Les Poésies de Peire Vidal.* Paris: Champion, 1913.

Ed. Appel   Appel, Carl (ed.). *Bernart von Ventadorn: Seine Lieder.* Halle: Niemeyer, 1915.

Ed. Canello   Canello, U. A. (ed.). *Arnaldo Daniello.* Halle: Niemeyer, 1883.

Ed. Kolsen   Kolsen, Adolf (ed.). *Giraut de Bornelh.* Halle: Niemeyer, 1910.

Ed. Rivalta   Rivalta, Ercole (ed.). *Le Rime di Guido Cavalcanti.* Bologna, 1922.

Monaci   Monaci, Ernesto. *Crestomazia italiana dei primi secoli.* Castello, 1912.

Opere   Barbi, M., *et al.* (eds.). *Le Opere di Dante, Testo critico della Societa Dantesca Italiana.* Firenze: Bemporad, 1921.

CHAPTER I

1. For example, Περὶ ὕψους, ix. 13.

2. *Republic* x. 602.

3. *Athenaeus* xi. 505b.

4. *Republic* x. 617 f.

5. *Gorgias* 523–24.

6. *Idea* ("Studien der Bibliothek Warburg," No. 5 [Leipzig, 1924]), pp. 1–16.

7. Cf. George Finsler, *Platon und die aristotelische Poetik* (Leipzig, 1900).

8. Cf. Eduard Norden, *Die Geburt des Kindes* ("Studien der Bibliothek Warburg," No. 3 [Leipzig, 1924]).

9. Recently adduced by Eduard Meyer, *Ursprung und Anfang des Christentums* (Stuttgart and Berlin, 1921–23), III, 219.

10. "Die Verklärungsgeschichte Jesu, der Bericht des Paulus (I Cor. 15: 3 ff.) und die beiden Christusvisionen des Petrus" (*Sitzungsbericht der Preussischen Akademie der Wissenschaften, Phil.-Hist. Klasse,* 1922).

11. St. Augustine, "Vorwort," *Reflexionen und Maximen* (Tübingen, 1922), p. v.

12. *Kunstgeschichte als Geistesgeschichte* (Munich, 1924), pp. 41 ff. (first appeared in *Historische Zeitschrift,* CXIX [1918]).

13. Cf. F. Neumann, "Wolfram von Eschenbachs Ritterideal," *Deutsche Vierteljahrsschrift für Litteraturwissenschaft und Geistesgeschichte,* V (1927), 9 ff.

14. *Die grossen Trobadors* (Munich, 1924), p. 48.

CHAPTER II

1. Cf. Karl Vossler, *Die Göttliche Komödie* (Heidelberg, 1925), II, 395–432.

2. *Deutsche Vierteljahrsschrift für Litteraturwissenschaft und Geistesgeschichte,* v. 1 (1927), 65 ff.

3. Cf. Monaci, No. 104, p. 303.

4. Recently a highly ingenious and logical attempt has been made by Luigi Valli in *Il Linguaggio segreto de Dante e dei "Fedeli d'Amore"* (Rome, 1928). But I do not believe that his book disproves my statement. Cf. the remarks of Benedetto Croce in his review of a book by Mauclair in *Critica* (September, 1928) and my discussion of it in *Deutsche Literaturzeitung* (1928), pp. 1357 ff.

5. *Opere,* p. 64.

6. *Vita nuova* xx.

7. *Opere,* p. 152.

8. *Inf.* iv. 97 ff.

9. *Purg.* xi. 98 ff.

10. *Purg.* ii.

11. *Par.* viii.

12. *Purg.* xxiv. 49 ff.

13. *Vita nuova* xxvi.

14. Translation by Dante G. Rossetti.

15. Monaci, No. 103.

16. Ed. Rivalta, p. 108.

17. Translation by Dante G. Rossetti.

18. Cf. on the following a criticism of Guinizelli's first poem in G. Lisio, *L'arte del periodo nelle opere volgari di Dante Alighieri* (Bologna, 1902), p. 54, and a comparison of the sonnets of Dante and Cavalcanti in Vossler, *op. cit.,* II, 561, who has also translated both poems into German.

19. Monaci, p. 301.

20. *Vita nuova* xxi.

21. Guinizelli: *ancor ve dico c'ha mazor vertute:*
                nul hom po mal pensar fin che la vede.

    Dante: *encor l'ha Dio per maggior grazia dato*
                che non po mal finir chi l'ha parlato.

    And God has bestowed on her this greater grace
    that he who has spoken to her cannot
    die in a state of sin.

22. *Vita nuova* xxiii.

23. *Opere*, p. 169.

24. *Ibid.*, p. 95.

25. *Ibid.*, p. 71.

26. *Ibid.*, p. 103.

27. I am thinking of the speech of Pia de' Tolomei (*Purg.* v. 130). Closely related to the apostrophe is the conjuration (*Se mai continga . . .*). It is not addressed to anyone in particular but conjures up, in desire or horror, the image of a non-existent condition. Again I am reminded of Homer with his ὡς ἀπόλοιτο καὶ ἄλλος (*Odyssey* i. 47) or the merry αἴ γὰρ τοῦτο γένοιτο (*Odyssey* viii. 339) and of other still more drastic passages in ancient poetry. This rhetorical form was also re-created by Dante; though it occurs occasionally in the medieval literature preceding him (for nearly every optative form is related to it and distinguished only in degree), it was he who first gave it suggestive power and concrete plasticity. The Provençal poets use it occasionally; I have been struck in Bernard de Ventadour by *Ja Deus nom don aquel poder* (ed. Appel, p. 85), or *Ai Deus! car se fosson trian* (ed. Appel, p. 186), and also by a few instances in Peire d'Alvernhe. It does not occur at all in Guinizelli and the first poets of the *stil nuovo;* Dante himself scarcely used it in the *Vita nuova;* only the pilgrim sonnet (xl) has something remotely like it. A few passages in the canzoni, for example, *Così nel mio parlar* (*Opere*, p. 107, 1. 53) and the fine sentence of *Convivio* i. III, *Ahi piaciuto fosse . . .* may be mentioned; but the form is not really developed until the *Comedy*.

28. Ed. Appel, p. 249.

29. Ed. Kolsen, No. 54, p. 342.

30. Ed. Anglade, p. 60.

31. *De vulgari eloquentia* ii. v.

32. Ed. Langfors, *Annales du Midi*, XXVI, 45; Lommatzsch, *Provenzalisches Liederbuch* (Berlin, 1917), p. 159.

33. Monaci, No. 104, p. 303.

34. Ed. Kolsen, No. 58, p. 374; Appel, *Provenzalische Chrestomathie*, No. 87.

35. Monaci, No. 103, p. 299.

36. *Vita nuova* xx.

37. Monaci, pp. 298 and 300.

38. *. . . non perch'io creda sua laude finire, ma ragionar per isfogar la mente.*

39. From the canzone *Li occhi dolenti* (*Vita nuova* xxxi).

40. *Vita nuova* xxi.

41. Vossler uses it (*op. cit.*, II, 433).

42. Wilamowitz' opinion.

43. The original passage in Dante is as follows: *Est, ut videtur, congrua (constructio) quam sectamur. Sed non minoris difficultatis accedit discretio prius quam, quam querimus, attingamus, videlicet urbanitate plenis-*

simam. Sunt etenim gradus constructionum quam plures: videlicet insipidus, qui est rudium; ut, Petrus amat multum dominam Bertam. Est et pure sapidus, qui est rigidorum scolarium vel magistrorum, ut, piget me, cunctis pietate maiorem, quicunque in exilio tabescentes patriam tantum sompniando revisunt. Est et sapidus et venustus, qui est quorundam superficietenus rhetoricam aurientium, ut, Laudabilis discretio marchionis Estensis et sua magnificentia preparata cunctis illum facit esse dilectum. Est et sapidus et venustus etiam et excelsus, qui est dictatorum illustrium, ut, Eiecta maxima parte florum de sinu tuo, Florentia, nequicquam Trinacriam Totila secundus adivit. Hunc gradum constructionis excellentissimum nominamus, et hic est quem querimus, cum suprema venemur, ut dictum est. Hoc solum illustres contiones inveniuntur contexte; ut Gerardus, Si per mon Sobretots non fos . . . . Nec mireris, lector, de tot reductis autoribus ad memoriam: non enim hanc quam suppremam vocamus constructionem nisi per huiusmodi exampla possumus indicare. Et fortassis utilissimum foret ad illam habituandam regulatos vidisse poetas, Virgilium videlicet, Ovidium Metamorfoseos, Statium atque Lucanum, nec non alios qui usi sunt altissimas prosas, ut titum Livium, Plinium, Frontinum, Paulum Orosium, et multos alios, quos amica solitudo nos visitare invitat. Subsistant igitur ignorantie sectatores Guittonem Aretinum et quosdam alios extollentes, nunquam in vocabulis atque constructione plebescere desuetos.

44. *Die Antike Kunstprosa* (Leipzig: Teubner, 1898), II, 753.

45. Vossler, *op. cit.*, II, 437 f.

46. *Ibid.*, p. 436.

47. It should be noted that this classification is only approximate. When Bernard de Ventadour writes: *Tout m'a mo cor e tout m'a me, e se mezeis e tot lo mon; e can se•m tolc, no•m laisset re, mas dezirer e cor volon* (ed. Appel, p. 249), he is coming very close to the dialectic of feeling.

48. *Purg.* xxvi. 117.

49. Ed. Canello, p. 102.

50. Ed. Kolsen, No. 53, p. 334.

51. Ed. Canello, p. 16.

52. *Ibid.*, p. 115.

53. Monaci, p. 301.

54. *Opere*, p. 202.

55. Ed. Rivalta, p. 130.

56. *Inf.* x. 52 ff.

57. *Opere*, p. 85.

58. *Par.* xvii. 69.

CHAPTER III

1. *Convivio* iv. xxvi.

2. Alois Dempf, *Die Hauptform mittelalterlicher Weltanschauung* (Munich and Berlin, 1925).

3. *Opere*, p. 192.

4. End of the canzone *Voi che 'ntendendo* (*Opere*, p. 171).

5. I prefer to assign the poems for Donna Pietra to a later period, although Michele Barbi, editor of the *Canzoniere*, is not of that opinion (*Opere*, p. xii). Apart from that, I have followed the order given the *Rime* in this edition—which strikes me as well chosen.

6. Beautifully described by Étienne Gilson in *Le Thomisme* ("Études de philosophie médiévale," No. 1) (Paris, 1922), p. 230: *une sorte de marge nous tient quelque peu en deça de notre propre définition, aucun de nous ne réalise plénièrement l'essence humaine ni même la notion complète de sa propre individualité.*

7. i. ii. (*Opere*, p. 151).

8. Cf. Wolfgang Seiferth's fine article, "Zur Kunstlehre Dantes," *Archiv für Kulturgeschichte*, XVII (1927).

9. *Che la bontà de l'animo, la quale questo servigio attende, è in coloro che per malvagia disusanza del mondo hanno lasciata la litteratura a coloro che l'hanno fatta di donna meretrice; e questi nobili sono principi, baroni, cavalieri, a molt' altra nobile gente, non solamente maschi ma femmine, che sono molti e molte in questa lingua, volgari, e non litterati. Convivio* i. ix (*Opere*, p. 161).

10. iv. xx (*Opere*, p. 290).

11. *Convivio* iv. xxvi. The source of these interpretations is probably the *Continentia Virgiliana* of Fulgentius.

12. *La Escatologia musulmana en la Divina Comedia* (Madrid, 1919); cf. the remarks of D. Scheludko in *Neuphilosophische Mitteilungen*, vol. XXVIII (1927).

13. *Convivio* ii. x (xL) after Boethius, *De consolatione philosophiae* i. ii. pr. 1.

14. One need only consider such episodes as those related by Robert Davidsohn in *Forschungen zur Geschichte von Florenz* (Berlin, 1896–1908), III, 66 f., 69, 72, 89.

15. On the objections recently raised to Dante's Thomism, cf. Giovanni Busnelli, S.J., *Cosmogonia e antropogenesi secondo Dante Alighieri e le sue fonti* (Rome, 1922).

16. *Unde dicendum est, quod distinctio rerum et multitudo est ex intentione primi agentis, quod est Deus. Produxit emim res in esse proper suam bonitatem communicandam creaturis et per eas repraesentandam: et quia per unam creaturam sufficienter repraesentari non potest, produxit multas creaturas et diversas, ut quod deest uni ad repraesentandam divinam bonitatem, suppleatur ex alia. Nam bonitas quae in Deo est simpliciter et uniformiter, in creaturis est multipliciter et divisim: unde perfectius participat divinam bonitatem et repraesentat eam totum universum quam alia quaecumquae creatura. Summa theologica* i. 47. 1. The translation given in the text is by the Fathers of the English Dominican Province (New York: Benziger, 1947), I, 246 (hereafter cited as Dominican Fathers Translation). Cf. also *Summa contra gentiles* ii. 45. A characteristic variant of the idea is

found in St. Bonaventure, II *Sent.* 18. 2. ad. 3^m and in II *Sent.* 3. 1. 2. 1 ad 2^m, quoted by Gilson, *La philosophie de Saint Bonaventure* (Paris, 1924), p. 308. St. Bonaventure speaks here only of the *multiplicatio numeralis*.

17. *Convivio* iv. XII. 14 ff.

18. Cf. also *Monarchia* i. XII (XIV). 1–5 (*Opere*, pp. 364 f.).

19. *Summa theologica* iii. *suppl.* 69. 2 *ad resp.* and *ad* 4. Cf. also *ibid.* i. IIae 4. 5 *ad resp.* (*sed circa*) and *ad* 5.

20. Line 103 ff.

21. *Summa theologica* i. IIae 4. 5 *ad* 2 (Dominican Fathers Translation, I, 606).

22. *Purg.* iii. 31 ff. and XXXV. 79 ff.; cf. Busnelli, *op. cit.*, pp. 204 ff. and 275 ff.

23. *Summa theologica* iii. *suppl.* 69. 1.

24. On the position of Augustine and St. Thomas, cf. Busnelli, *op. cit.*, pp. 288 ff., particularly p. 292, n. 1.

25. Line 673. In this connection "un-Dantesque" means only incompatible with the vision of the other world set forth in the *Comedy*. The words *loco certo non c'è posto* (no definite place is assigned to us), spoken by Sordello (*Purg.* vii. 40), apply only to those waiting in Limbo.

26. Line 743. Eduard Norden, quite in keeping with our interpretation, translates "suos manes" as "his daemon." *P. Vergilius Maro, Aeneis Buch VI, erklärt von Ed. Norden* (1916), p. 95: *Ein jeder büsst, wie es sein Dämon heischt.*

27. Lines 463–4:

> *. . . nec credere quivi*
> *ec hunc tantum tibi me discessu ferre dolorem.*

28. *Summa theologica* i. 118. 2 *ad* 2 *et ideo dicendum: Quando perfectior forma advenit, fit corruptio prioris; ita tamen, quod sequens forma habet, quicquid habebat prima, et adhuc amplius* (Dominican Fathers Translation, I, 575).

29. See pp. 2 ff. above.

30. Formulated, for example, by Vincent of Beauvais, *Speculum doctrinale*, lib. III, chap. 109.

31. Letter to Can Grande (*Opere*, p. 439).

32. *Inf.* XX. 113.

33. *Ibid.*

34. *Par.* XXV. 1; XXIII. 62; XVII. 128.

35. Horace, *Epistles* ii. 3. 127 (*De arte poetica*).

36. Cf. Friedrich Rintelen, *Giotto* (Basle, 1923); E. Rosenthal, *Giotto in der mittelalterlichen Geistensentwicklung* (Augsburg, 1924); M. Dvôràk, *Geschichte der Italienschen Malerei* (1927), pp. 13 ff.; A. Schmarsow, *Italienische Kunst im Zeitalter Dantes* (1928).

37. Cf. Alois Dempf, *op. cit.*, pp. 159 ff.

38. Cf. Friedrich Gundolf, *Caesar, Geschichte seines Ruhms* (Berlin, 1925), pp. 99 ff.

39. See p. 77, n. 9 above.

40. Eclogue 1 of Giovanni del Virgilio (*Opere*, p. 455).

41. *Inf.* ii. 96.

CHAPTER IV

1. *Inf.* xxxiv. 106 ff.; Edward Moore, *Studies in Dante*, Series III, p. 119.

2. *In nobilissimo loco totius terrae* (*Summa theologica*. i. 102; i. *ad resp.*)
Cf. Moore, *op. cit.*, III, 136.

3. For a detailed treatment of the movements of the heavenly bodies, see
Moore, "The Astronomy of Dante," *op. cit.*, III.

4. *Par.* ii. 112 ff.

5. *Par.* xiii. 53.

6. *Par.* vii. 124 ff.

7. *Par.* vii. 109.

8. *Purg.* xvii. 91 ff. Cf. also *Convivio* ii. xiv. 14 ff., where the effect of the
motion of the *primum mobile* on nature is described.

9. *Par.* xiii. 58 ff.

10. *Par* i. 103 ff. Cf. *Summa theologica*. i. 59. 1 *ad resp.; Monarchia* i. 3.

11. *Purg.* xxx. 109 f.

12. *Par.* v. 19 ff.

13. *Corpora caelestia*, says St. Thomas, *non possunt esse per se causa
operationum liberi arbitrii; possunt tamen ad hoc dispositive inclinare in
quantum imprimunt in corpus humanum, et per consequens in vires sensi-
tivas quae sunt actus corporalium organorum, quae inclinant ad humanos
actus* (*Summa theologica* ii. iiae. 95.5 [Dominican Fathers Translation]).

14. *Corpora caelestia non sunt voluntatum neque electionum causa. Vo-
luntas enim in parte intellectiva animae est. . . . Corpora caelestia non possunt
imprimere directe in intellectum nostrum. . . .* (*Summa contra gentiles* iii.
85 [*Basic Writings of St. Thomas Aquinas,* ed. Anton C. Pegis (New York,
1945), II, 159]).

15. *Monarchia* i. iii.

16. *Purg.* xvii. 94. For an exposition of the physical system, see the works
of Edward Moore. Aside from those already mentioned above, see particularly: "The Geography of Dante," *op. cit.*, III, and "Dante's Theory of Creation," *op. cit.*, IV.

17. *Inf.* xv. 85.

18. Nevertheless, cf. *Inf.* iv. 76 ff. and particularly *Inf.* xiv. 63 ff.

19. *Amor propriae excellentiae in quantum ex amore causatur inordinata
praesumptio alios superandi* (*Summa theologica* ii. iiae. 162, 3 *ad* 4).

20. *Purg.* xvii. 91 ff.

21. In the present work it will be possible to set forth only the barest
outlines of Dante's ethical system. We shall neither be able to go very deeply
into its dogmatic foundations, nor to disentangle the intricate symbolic references, nor to discuss at any length the problems involved. From the abun-

dant literature I have endeavored to peel out the prevailing opinion, but I have not entirely succeeded in avoiding controversial statements and a certain arbitrariness in my choice of what to say and what to leave unsaid. Among the works that take a position differing from my own, I should like at least to mention Luigi Pietrobono's book, *Dal Centro al cerchio* (Turin, 1923). Starting from Lucifer and Cocytus, he builds up a unified ethical system for the whole poem, hence also for the *Inferno*. His work shows an admirable knowledge of Dante; the relationships and concordances it lays bare give an entirely new idea of the rich intellectual content of the *Comedy*.

22. *Inf.* iii. 36.

23. *Inf.* xxviii. 142.

24. *Scienza nuova,* ed. Nicollini, pp. 727, 733, 750; also Vico, *Opere,* ed. Ferrari (2d ed.), IV, 198 ff., and *ibid.*, VI, 34 ff. and 41 ff.

25. He believed that Dante would have been a greater poet if he had known nothing of Scholasticism or Latin (Vico, *op. cit.*, IV, 200).

26. *Inf.* ix. 34 ff. Consequently I believe that there is no justification for declining to explain this passage, as many commentators have done, on the ground that Dante meant nothing in particular, or that his meaning is unimportant or unpoetic, or that Virgil's words of adjuration are merely an artifice with which to introduce what follows, or that the words are a reference to the following passage. Dante means what he says, and although the *Comedy* is often difficult, it is not a mystification. Consequently, one must either explain such a passage or admit that one does not know the meaning. The art of interpretation is lost if one supposes that one is justified, in the name of a higher poetic insight, in neglecting the clear words of the text. It seems to me that a mythographical tradition harking back to Fulgentius provides a step toward an explanation. In Fulgentius the Gorgons signify *tria terroris genera* (three classes of terror) and Medusa the supreme degree of terror, *qui non solum mentis intentum, verum etiam caliginem ingerat visus* (which not only affects the mind, but also obscures the vision); this accounts for the name of Medusa (*mē-idousa,* unseeing). Perseus kills Medusa with the help of Minerva, *quia virtus, auxiliatrice sapientia, omnes terrores vincit* (because virtue with the help of wisdom overcomes all terrors) —so runs the paraphrase of Mythographus vaticanus secundus (ed. Bode, *Scriptores rerum mythicarum* [1834], p. 113, who surprisingly, after copying Fulgentius almost word for word, designates Medusa as *"oblivio"*—mental blindness or forgetfulness induced by excessive fear).

27. *Purg.* ix. 73 ff.

28. *Paradisus terrestris pertinet magis ad statum viatoris quam ad statum recipientis pro meritis; et ideo inter receptacula . . . (animarum) non computatur* (*Summa theologica* iii. suppl. 69. 7 ad 5).

29. *Purg.* xxi. 34 ff.

30. *Par.* vii. 130.

31. See Parodi, *Bulletin of the Society of Dante,* New Series, XXIII (1916), 150 ff.

32. *Par.* iv. 28 ff.

33. *Par.* xxx. 113.

34. See the plan in the edition of L. Olschki (Heidelberg, 1918), p. 523.

35. Cf. *Purg.* xix. 1–3.

36. *Par.* xxx. 129.

37. *Par.* vii. 19 ff.; also *Purg.* xxix. 24 ff. and *Par.* xxvi. 115 ff.

38. *Purg.* xxxii. 102.

39. *Par.* vi; *Inf.* xxxiv. 61 ff.; also *Purg.* xxi. 82 ff. and many other passages. This is also the place to mention Luigi Valli's new interpretation of the *Comedy,* inspired by Pascoli, which has quickly won fame by its astuteness and the concreteness of its exposition. According to Valli, the structure of the poem is based on a system of parallels between the symbols of the Cross and the Eagle, and even in respect to individual redemption he imputes to the Eagle equal significance with the Cross. Cf. Valli's two main works on the *Comedy: Il Segreto della croce e dell' aquila nella Divina commedia* (Bologna, 1922) and *La Chiave della Divina commedia* (Bologna, 1925); and also L. Pietrobono in *Giornale Dantesco,* XXX (1927), 89 ff.

40. *Purg.* xxxii.

41. *Proemio* of the *Istorie fiorentine.*

42. Guittone d'Arezzo in his Canzone *Ahi lasso! or è stagion di doler tanto* (*Rime,* ed. Pellegrini [Bologna, 1901], p. 316).

43. *Par.* v. 76 ff.

44. *Par.* xxx. 133 ff.

45. *Inf.* i. 94 ff.

46. *Purg.* xxxiii. 31 ff.

47. Cf. also *Par.* xxvii. 142 ff.

48. Alfred Bassermann, "Veltro, Gross-Chan und Kaisersage," *Neue Heidelberger Jahrbücher,* XI (1902); Franz Kampers, *Dante und die Wiedergeburt* (Mainz, 1921); Franz Kampers, *Vom Werdegang der abendländischen Kaisermystik* (Leipzig and Berlin, 1924), particularly pp. 141 f.; Konrad Burdach, *Reformation, Renaissance, Humanismus* (2d ed.; Berlin and Leipzig, 1926), especially pp. 57 ff.; and Konrad Burdach, "Dante und das Problem der Renaissance," *Deutsche Rundschau.* February-March, 1924.

49. *Mittelalterliche Studien,* Bd. I, Hft. 1 (Leipzig, 1913).

50. *Inf.* xiv. 76 ff.

51. Cf. Kern, *op. cit.,* pp. 88 ff.

52. Cf. *Par.* viii. 115 ff.

53. *Purg.* xxvii. 142.

CHAPTER V

1. *Inf.* xv.

2. *Purg.* xxi.

3. *Par.* viii.

4. *Inf.* x.

5. *Inf.* x. 22 ff.

6. *Inf.* xxvii. 19 ff.

7. *Purg.* vi.

8. *Inf.* xxvii.

9. *Mal volontier lo dico; ma sforzami la tua chiara favella, che mi fa sovvenir del mondo antico* (Unwillingly I tell it, but your clear speech, that makes me recollect the former world, compels me). *Inf.* xviii. 52 ff.

10. *Inf.* xxvii. 67.

11. *Purg.* v. 130 ff.

12. *Inf.* xviii. 55 ff.

13. *Scienza nuova,* ed. Nicollini, pp. 750 ff.

14. *Par.* xvii. 136 ff.

15. Friedrich Gundolf, *Caesar, Geschichte seines Ruhms,* pp. 99 ff.

16. *Inf.* iv. 86.

17. *Inf.* xxvi.

18. Manfredi Porena, *Delle manifestazioni plastiche del sentimento nei personaggi della Divina commedia* (Milan, 1902).

19. *Purg.* xxxi. 68.

20. *Inf.* xxxii. 12.

21. *Inf.* xiii.

22. *Inf.* xxiv. 25.

23. See pp. 110–11 above.

24. *Par.* xxiii. 25.

25. *Par.* xxvii. 92.

26. *Inf.* vi. 19.

27. *Par.* xvii. 131.

28. *Par.* xvii. 120.

29. *L'Ile des Pingouins* (Paris, 1925), pp. 152 ff.

30. *Purg.* xvii. 13 ff.

31. *Bertram de Born,* ed. Albert Stimmung (2d ed.; Halle: Niemeyer, 1913), p. 54.

32. *Inf.* i. 7.

33. *Inf.* x. 124.

34. *Purg.* xxi. 113.

35. *Purg.* xxv. 17.

36. *Par.* xxxiii. 1–10.

37. *Par.* xvii. 34.

38. *Par.* xvii. 58.

39. *Par.* xxxii. 139.

40. *Inf.* ii. 59 f.

41. *Purg.* viii. 3.

42. *Inf.* xiii. 42.

43. *Inf.* ii. 13.

44. *Par.* xxiii. 61 ff.

45. *Par.* xxv. 1 ff.

46. *Inf.* iv. 1 ff.
47. Lisio, *op. cit.*, p. 163.
48. *Purg.* iii. 107.
49. *Inf.* xxxiii. 150.
50. *Purg.* xv. 109.
51. *Purg.* iii. 103.
52. *Inf.* xxvii. 110.
53. *Inf.* v. 103.
54. *Par.* xx. 98.
55. *Par.* xxix. 26.
56. *Inf.* ii. 3.
57. *Purg.* v. 100.
58. Vandelli's critical text has a semicolon after *parola*. See *Opere*, p. 617.
59. *Inf.* ii. 5.
60. *Inf.* iii. 31.

CHAPTER VI

1. Preface to the *Dante Uebertragungen*.

INDEX

Achilles, 1, 2
Adam, 121
Aeneas, 81, 89
Agathon, 9
Albertus Magnus, 101
Albrecht, Kaiser, 128
Alfraganus, 101
Amore, 27 ff., 35, 60, 72, 113
Anchises, 89
Ancona, Alessandro d', 81
Andreas Capellanus, 48
Antigone, 142
Apology, 6
Aquinas, St. Thomas, 71, 73 ff., 84–
   87, 91, 94–95, 101, 103–5, 107, 114,
   120
Arezzo, d'. *See* Guittone d'Arezzo
Argenti, 152
Aristophanes, 9, 146
Aristotle, 7–9, 76, 87, 101, 105, 109
Arnaut Daniel. *See* Daniel, Arnaut
Asín Palacios, 81
Augustine, St., 17, 71, 76

Babylon, 128
Bardi, Simone de', 60
Bassermann, Alfred, 129
Beatrice, 60 ff., 98, 99, 100, 115, 119,
   126, 127, 135, 152, 163
Belacqua, 152
Benedict, St., 119
Bernard, St., 38, 120, 163
Bernard de Ventadour, 26, 39, 51
Boethius, 71, 76
Bonagiunta da Lucca, 29, 45
Bonaventure, St., 120
Boniface VIII (Pope), 65
Borchardt, Rudolf, 22
Brunetto Latini, 75, 99, 105, 136
Brutus, 109, 123

Buonconte da Montefeltro, 114, 171
Burdach, Konrad, 129
Busnelli, Giovanni, 116

Cacciaguida, 75, 99, 149, 156, 172
Caesar, 96, 109, 147, 150
Canello, U. A., 53
Cangrande, 129
Capet, Hugh, 114
Casella, 29, 152, 172
Cassius, 109, 123
Cato, 96, 131, 150
Cavalcanti, Guido, 28 ff., 56, 58, 60,
   68, 72, 76, 138
Christ, 11, 18 ff., 121–23
Ciacco, 152
Cicero, 9, 71
Cimabue, 149
Cino da Pistoia, 28
Comedy, classical, 4, 14, 92, 146
Constantine, 123
Crito, 6

Damian, Peter, St., 119
Daniel, Arnaut, 22, 24, 51–52, 54, 114
De vulgari eloquentia, 49, 56
Demosthenes, 37
Dempf, Alois, 69
Dido, 81, 89
Dolce stil nuovo, 33 ff., 60, 68
Dominic, St., 120
Dvořák, M., 20

Eleaticism, 5
Epicureans, 9, 107
Eve, 121

Farinata degli Ulberti, 138
Fathers of the Church, 16, 87